THE OCEANS

Look for these and other books in the
Lucent Endangered Animals and Habitats Series:

The Elephant
The Giant Panda
The Oceans
The Rhinoceros
The Shark
The Whale

Other related titles in the Lucent Overview Series:

Acid Rain
Endangered Species
Energy Alternatives
Garbage
The Greenhouse Effect
Hazardous Waste
Ocean Pollution
Oil Spills
Ozone
Pesticides
Population
Rainforests
Recycling
Vanishing Wetlands
Zoos

THE OCEANS

BY LISA A. WROBLE

Endangered
Animals &
Habitats

LUCENT BOOKS, INC.
SAN DIEGO, CALIFORNIA

Library of Congress Cataloging-in-Publication Data

Wroble, Lisa A.
  The oceans / by Lisa A. Wroble.
    p.   cm. — (Endangered animals & habitats)
  Includes bibliographical references (p.   ) and index.
  Summary: Discusses the world's oceans as habitats endangered
by human pollution and examines efforts to counter the damage and
conserve them.
  ISBN 1-56006-464-1 (alk. paper)
  1. Marine ecology—Juvenile literature.   2. Endangered ecosystems—Juvenile literature.   3. Marine pollution—Juvenile literature.   4. Nature—Effect of human beings on—Juvenile literature.
[1. Marine pollution.   2. Marine ecology.   3. Pollution.   4. Ecology.]   I. Title.   II. Series.
QH541.5.S3W76   1998
577.7—dc21   97-27275
                                                              CIP
                                                              AC

Contents

INTRODUCTION   6

CHAPTER ONE   8
The Ocean in the Global Ecosystem

CHAPTER TWO   15
A Natural Resource

CHAPTER THREE   25
Harvesting the Ocean

CHAPTER FOUR   38
Polluting the Ocean

CHAPTER FIVE   54
The Coastal Zone

CHAPTER SIX   67
The Ocean's Future

GLOSSARY   81
ORGANIZATIONS TO CONTACT   84
SUGGESTIONS FOR FURTHER READING   88
WORKS CONSULTED   89
INDEX   92
PICTURE CREDITS   96
ABOUT THE AUTHOR   96

Introduction

THE WORLD OCEAN, which is huge, covers nearly three-quarters of the globe. For centuries, human beings have turned to this vast, wild resource to provide food, clothing, and other items, such as sponges and salt. The ocean also fills the atmosphere with oxygen, just as trees do. It is hard to imagine that such a broad and powerful force in life could ever be at risk. Yet, without proper care and management, the ocean is a limited resource that can be depleted.

The ocean is the final stop for much of the garbage and pollution generated on land. Polluted rivers and streams drain into the ocean. Waste management officials dump containers of chemical waste on the deep, cold ocean bottom, and sewage processing centers release billions of gallons of treated waste water into the ocean. It has been determined that oil tankers flush oil-holding compartments and fisheries dump scrap parts and unwanted or spoiled fish back into the ocean waters. Once this pollution is in the ocean, it has nowhere else to go.

As the ocean becomes more polluted, marine life suffers and dies. Some creatures are poisoned by eating food coated with crude oil. Others strangle or suffocate on plastic garbage. Breeding grounds are also destroyed to make land available for resorts or houses on the coastlines. With more young fish dying from pollution, those harvested for food are not being replaced.

The ocean's other resources are also being stripped. Products such as minerals, sponges, gravel, and sand are removed. Coral and other items are taken for souvenirs. The removal of these things destroys the environment of many ocean species. As a result, marine plants and animal species weaken and die; the ocean struggles to recover the losses.

As human population grows, demand on the ocean's resources will also grow. Marine specialists assert that the ocean is not being given time to replenish these resources before more are taken. Others argue that we cannot afford to wait, or that the ocean is so huge that other areas for catching fish and for mining gravel and sand can be found.

A bird struggles for survival after being soaked with oil that was accidentally released into the ocean.

Environmentalists believe that steps should be taken now to reverse pollution and replace damaged habitats. Some experts predict that given humankind's present course, in twenty years the only fish to harvest will not be worth eating. Similarly, the costs of finding and harvesting uncontaminated sand and gravel will outweigh the benefit.

The biggest factor, however, is time. It will take time for water quality to improve, for breeding grounds and habitats to flourish again, and for many marine species to restock themselves.

The ocean's ability to restore itself can be strengthened. But these efforts cost money and require changes in the way people do things. Experts differ on how laws governing ocean use should be changed and how the changed laws should be enforced. Since the ocean is shared by all countries, the responsibility for saving it is global. This enormous task raises many questions. Can people work together in saving the ocean's resources? Can developing countries pay the cost for cleanup and changing regulations?

If not, who will?

1

The Ocean in the Global Ecosystem

AS LAND DWELLERS, human beings tend to focus most of their attention on the dry parts of their world. Even the name of our planet—Earth—reflects the human fascination with the land. A quick look at a world map, however, shows that water, not land, dominates the surface of the planet. Water covers more than 72 percent of the globe. Color photographs of the world taken from outer space dramatize this fact. Bathed in the sun's light, planet Earth gleams blue.

When people do think about water, they usually are concerned with freshwater—the liquid they drink, bathe in, and use to wash their clothes. Freshwater is necessary for human life, but it makes up only a fraction of the water on the planet. Only 3 percent of the world's water is contained in freshwater bodies such as lakes, rivers, streams, and ponds. The vast majority of the world's water—97 percent of it—is contained in four huge bodies of saltwater known as the oceans. One of the oceans—the Pacific Ocean—is large enough in volume to hold all the world's landmass.

A close look at a world map reveals that the world's four oceans are connected. The smallest of the oceans, the Arctic, meets the largest ocean, the Pacific, at a point between North America and Asia known as the Bering Strait. Farther east, the Arctic Ocean joins the second-largest ocean, the Atlantic, off the coasts of Greenland and northern Europe. The Atlantic Ocean, in turn, flows into the Pacific Ocean off the southernmost tip of South America and into the third-largest ocean, the Indian Ocean, off the tip of Africa. The Pacific Ocean joins the Indian Ocean off the coasts of Australia. As the Portuguese explorer Ferdinand Magellan proved nearly five hundred years ago, it is possible to travel around the entire globe without ever touching land. The world's four oceans are in fact one large body of water—the global ocean.

Ocean motion

Unlike water in a pond, the waters of the global ocean do not stand still. Currents keep the ocean waters in constant motion around the planet. Pushed along by ocean currents, a single drop of water could, like Magellan, circumnavigate the globe. Progress would be slow, however. Scientists estimate it would take about five thousand years for a drop of water to circle the Earth.

Some currents are like deep-sea streams, pushing through the surrounding waters like a river carving its way through land. Other currents are more subtle. They move

A photograph of Earth taken from outer space shows the surface of the planet to be mostly covered with water.

masses of water so gradually that their motion is barely detectable to human observers. To map the movements of currents, oceanographers—scientists who study the ocean—have placed buoys loaded with instruments in the world's ocean at various points around the globe. These buoys measure and record the temperature and movement of the water around them. They also measure atmospheric conditions such as air temperature and wind speeds. These measurements tell oceanographers a great deal about the movement of currents.

Another way to observe the actions of a current is to watch and measure the movement of objects floating in the water. For example, oceanographers were able to learn a great deal about currents when a cargo ship lost crates of Nike shoes during a storm in the Pacific. Within weeks, Nike shoes began washing ashore in Washington and Oregon. People created the Sneaker Society to meet and try to find matching pairs of shoes. As the shoes began to beach on shores farther and farther away from the storm area, scientists recorded how long it took for the shoes to reach distant shores. Michael Weber, formerly on the staffs of the Center for Marine Conservation and the National Marine

A stretch of shoreline along the west coast of the United States. Scientists were able to learn more about ocean currents when a load of sneakers fell into the water off this coast and drifted ashore.

Fisheries Service, and Judith A. Gradwohl, director of the Smithsonian Institution's Environmental Awareness Program, noted in their book *The Wealth of Oceans*, "The Nike shoe spill was the largest release of human-made drift objects ever, and therefore the largest experiment for charting the ocean surface currents."

What causes currents?

Through observation, oceanographers have discovered that many factors affect the formation and actions of currents. The weather above the ocean's surface is one such factor. The trade winds, which blow in one direction for long periods of time, push surface water along. Unseen forces, such as gravity, can also affect the motion of the water. As the earth rotates, its gravity pulls the great masses of water at its surface along with it. This gravitational force subtly stirs the waters from within. Even the gravity of the moon and the sun causes the waters of the ocean to move.

One of the most powerful forces that drives the currents is the energy of the sun. Heat from the sun warms the water near the surface of the ocean. As the water warms, it expands, pushing outward against the cooler waters around it. This pressure causes the cooler waters to move. When water cools, the opposite occurs; it contracts. The contraction of cool water leaves a void that warmer waters rush to fill. Since the earth's equator is closer to the sun than its poles are, the water near it warms up more than the water farther away from it does. As a result, the equatorial waters are constantly pushing outward against the cooler waters to the north and south.

The shape of the ocean floor also affects currents. If the depth of the ocean were uniform, its waters would heat up and cool down at relatively the same rate. As a result, the pressures exerted by the warming and cooling water would remain relatively constant. The ocean floor, however, is far from flat. Like the land above, the ocean floor contains mountains, plains, valleys, and canyons. Because of the contours beneath the surface, the depth of the water varies greatly from one part of the ocean to another. The water is shallow in some places and deep in others. The uneven depth of the water creates an uneven pattern of heating and cooling. Shallow water, which is close to the surface, heats up quickly. Deep water heats up more slowly. These differences in the temperatures of the water create differences in its pressures, causing even more motion.

Climate regulator

Just as weather affects the temperature and movements of the ocean, so, too, do the temperature and movement of ocean water affect the weather. The main reason for this is the different rates at which air and water heat up and cool down. In summer months, the ocean absorbs heat from the sun. Land also absorbs heat, but the ocean heats up at a much slower rate than land does. If the earth were made up of more land and less water, the global climate would be much hotter. Likewise, if the Pacific Ocean were smaller, the land areas surrounding it would be much hotter. Because the earth has three times as much water as land, the ocean is able to absorb much of the sun's heat. This keeps the earth from becoming too hot to support life.

In winter months the ocean releases its heat. Currents of the ocean aid in sending heated masses of water to other parts of the globe. In the Gulf of Mexico, off Florida's coast, for example, a mass of saltwater absorbs heat. The current then carries this mass of warmed water to northern Europe. The warmth is released into the air, helping to regulate the temperature of the continent.

Rainmaker

Without the ocean, the cycle of evaporation, condensation, and precipitation would also be greatly reduced. Since the waters of the global ocean are always in motion, the water has no place else to go except around the globe. The only outlet it has is through evaporation.

As the sun heats the ocean, some of the surface water evaporates. This water vapor enters the air. About 85 percent of the atmosphere contains water vapor from the ocean. When the water becomes vapor, the salt and other impuri-

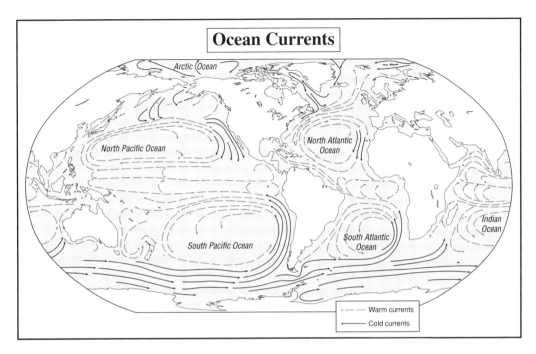

Ocean Currents

Arctic Ocean

North Pacific Ocean

North Atlantic Ocean

Indian Ocean

South Pacific Ocean

South Atlantic Ocean

- - - - Warm currents
——— Cold currents

ties are left behind. For this reason, the surface water of the tropical areas, where the sun is hotter and evaporates the water at a faster rate, is much saltier than the surface water of the Arctic areas, where the water evaporates more slowly.

The water vapor travels through the atmosphere on air currents. As air currents cool the water vapor, it condenses into drops of liquid water. Clouds form from this condensed water. As the clouds cool more, the condensed water is released through precipitation—rain or snow.

The world's freshwater supply is renewed by precipitation. The evaporation and condensation process removes the salt and impurities from the rainwater. Thus, ocean water is recycled by nature into drinkable freshwater. For example, of the roughly thirty inches of rainfall in the United States per day (or 4.2 trillion gallons), one-third finds its way to streams, rivers, and groundwater supplies.

This map of ocean currents reveals how the waters of the global ocean constantly move across the surface of the planet.

Ocean ecosystem

Many different plants, fish, mammals, and other organisms make up the ocean habitat. The ocean habitat, as a whole, is made up of many separate ecosystems. An ecosystem is a group of living things—both plant and animal—and nonliving things like soil and rocks that rely on each other for survival. The nonliving, or physical, parts, in relation to the living parts, make up a unique environment. All the pieces are interrelated and necessary for the group to function together as an ecosystem. The Great Barrier Reef off the coast of Australia and the giant kelp forests off the coast of California are examples of ocean ecosystems.

A distinct group of marine species exists within each of these ecosystems. Most but not all of these creatures spend their entire lives within the ecosystem and could not survive outside of it. A few marine species cross from one ecosystem to another for shelter or food, but their stays are usually temporary. For instance, a baby whale may swim into a kelp forest to hide from sharks, but it will not live there permanently. Similarly, some octopuses lay their eggs in the protection of a coral reef's cavelike cavities, but once the babies hatch, they move into open water. Just as the world's four oceans are connected and form one global ocean, so, too, are the ocean's separate ecosystems connected, surviving within the greater ecosystem of the global ocean habitat.

Global ecosystem

Huge as it is, the global ocean is part of an even larger ecosystem—the global ecosystem. The ocean currents are shaped by the forces of the atmosphere as well as the contours of the landmass. The world's weather is influenced by different rates of heating and cooling of the atmosphere above both water and land. Oxygen, key to life on the planet, is produced by the plants that live in the ocean as well as by trees and other vegetation on land.

As part of the global system, human beings are influenced not only by the forces on land, but also those far out to sea. A temperate atmosphere, freshwater, oxygen—all of these elements—are vital to human survival. Without the global ocean, life as it is presently known would not exist.

2

A Natural Resource

MOST SCIENTISTS NOW believe that human beings first developed as a species in central Africa. From there, early humans migrated through the rest of Africa and into Australia, Asia, Europe, and North and South America. Many of these early cultures settled near oceans because of the wealth of food and other supplies they could obtain from the watery depths. The global ocean is not only the largest geographic feature of the planet, but also the richest in natural resources. Throughout human history millions of people have used the ocean's resources to survive and thrive.

Food from the sea

One of the main resources the ocean provides is food. Fish of all varieties and shellfish such as oysters, shrimp, lobster, and crab are harvested and eaten worldwide. In fact, seafood makes up one-sixth of the animal protein consumed by human beings. Three nations—China, Japan, and the United States—alone consume more than 37 million metric tons of seafood per year. In most industrialized nations, seafood makes up a small part of the diet. In these countries, people eat seafood mainly for variety. In Third World countries, however, seafood is a staple. People in these nations rely on seafood for 40 percent of their protein.

Not all of the fish people harvest ends up on the dining table. Much of it is fed to animals. Menhaden is a type of small fish ground into meal used in animal food. Fish oil is also used in industrial processes.

Rich in vitamins and minerals, seaweed is eaten by many people around the world.

People also consume plants from the sea. Seaweed—including kelp, sea lettuce, and Irish moss—is popular in many countries. A type of algae, seaweed absorbs vitamins and minerals from the ocean water. Because seaweed is rich in these compounds, it is also ground into protein powders to be used as food supplements and as bodybuilding aids.

Seaweed is also used in the making of processed foods and drugs. It is hard to imagine many people rushing to the store to buy seaweed ice cream, but a jellylike substance found in underwater plants is now being used as a natural thickener in popular frozen desserts. Seaweed jellies are also used in cosmetic and pharmaceutical products to create a smooth texture and help retain moisture.

At some point in the distant past, people noticed that when objects from the ocean, such as seaweed, wash ashore and dry, they are coated with a white, granular substance. This white residue is made up mainly of salt, a mineral valued for its ability to enhance the flavor of cooked food. People learned centuries ago that they could harvest salt from the ocean by filling shallow bins with seawater and leaving them in the sun to dry. After the water evaporated, the salt left was used, traded, or sold.

Most of the table salt used today comes from underground mines. The salt in these mines was left by ocean water that receded from land long ago. Some salt is still taken from ocean water through evaporation. This salt is usually called solar salt. Commercial solar saltworks remove salt from ocean water using a series of evaporating ponds. As the water moves through the ponds, it becomes separated from trace minerals such as potassium and calcium. By the time the water reaches the final evaporating pond, only table salt remains.

Clothing

The first people to settle by the ocean no doubt did so because it was a never-ending source of food. They soon discovered, however, that marine life provided a wealth of other products as well. For example, early humans found that the skins of ocean-dwelling mammals can be used to make clothing. For centuries, people in cold climates have prized the coats of seals, sea lions, whales, and walruses for their warmth and durability. Today, the Inuit and other Arctic tribes still dress in garments made from these creatures. Even the skins of large fish, such as sharks, have been used to make clothing.

A sea of riches

The flesh and skins of marine animals are not the only body parts that people have used through the ages. The teeth and bones of sea animals have proven to be vital resources as well. For thousands of years, people made knives, clubs, axes, hammers, and other tools from the bones of whales and the tusks of walruses. Hunters found that shark teeth made good arrowheads. Garment makers used fish bones for sewing needles. During the nineteenth century, whalebone was sewn between layers of fabric to make corsets for women.

The soft, inner skeleton of another sea creature—the sponge—also proved useful to people. Sponges are marine animals that live on the ocean floor and attach themselves to rocks, plants, and other objects. About five thousand species of sponges live in the ocean—mainly in warm, shallow waters. People discovered centuries ago that when a sponge dies, its hard outer cells can be removed, leaving behind a soft material called spongin. Since spongin absorbs large amounts of water, it is ideal for cleaning and bathing. Today, most sponges used for cleaning are made with synthetic materials. Artificial sponges are cheap to produce and often last longer than natural sponges. Many people still prefer natural sponges for bathing, however. Commercial fishing boats harvest sponges from the waters of the Gulf Stream and the Mediterranean Sea.

Artists and artisans also use materials from the ocean to make jewelry and other decorative items. Because of the unusual colors and patterns they sometimes contain, seashells have been used around the world to make jewelry, buttons,

These red vase sponges grow in the waters of the Caribbean Sea. People use natural sponges like these for bathing and cleaning.

and other trinkets. For centuries, artists have made intricate carvings on whale teeth and walrus tusks. These carvings, known as scrimshaw, have been applied to rings, earrings, and pendants, as well as freestanding objects of art.

Probably the most valuable items—ounce for ounce—produced in the ocean are pearls. Raw pearls form when a foreign body, such as a grain of sand, works its way inside a pearl oyster. The oyster emits a whitish fluid which encases the object. Eventually, the milky substance hardens. As long as the oyster lives, it will continue to coat the foreign object with layer after layer of fluid. Eventually, the layers build up, forming a hard sphere—a pearl. Prized for their beauty, natural pearls are treated as gems in the making of fine jewelry. Divers still harvest raw pearls from the ocean floor, but most pearls are now grown in commercial oyster beds. In these commercial operations, foreign objects are intentionally planted inside the oysters. Pearls formed in this way are known as cultured pearls.

Pearls are an animal by-product that appeal to the human eye. Less attractive but still valuable is another by-product of marine life—guano. Guano is composed of the droppings of seabirds such as pelicans, penguins, petrels, gannets, and cormorants. Since these birds eat fish, their droppings are rich in nitrogen and phosphate. As a result, guano makes an excellent plant fertilizer. Islands off the coasts of Peru and Ecuador are main sources of guano. At one time, these islands held guano deposits that were one hundred feet thick.

Medical research

Just as the minerals in guano can be used to strengthen growing plants, so can other ocean compounds be used to improve the health of human beings. In the twentieth century, marine biologists—scientists who study ocean life—learned a great deal about the medicinal potential of ocean plants and animals. They found that many of the minerals and enzymes found in marine life can promote healing. For example, some researchers believe that enzymes and chemicals in shark tissue can be used in the treatment of cancer and AIDS. Sharks are also being used in antiviral research, as is seaweed. Substances in sponges are being tested for use in the fight against leukemia.

Recently, marine biologists saw a way to exploit the similarity between human bone and coral. Like bone, coral is porous. Furthermore, when coral is treated with heat, it changes into the same mineral that makes up bone. Because of these similarities, doctors have begun to use coral in the grafting of human bones. After the bone and the coral are joined, the blood vessels in the bone are able to find a path through the maze of pores in the coral. As a result, a solid bond grows between the healthy bone and the coral. Normally, when bone needs to be filled in, grafts are taken from the patient's ribs, hip, or skull. By using coral instead, doctors can eliminate the need for additional incisions. This reduces the amount of pain for the patient and decreases the risk of infection.

Just as the study of coral has resulted in finding similarities between it and human bone, studying jellyfish has helped scientists

In a coral bone graft, surgeons replace a section of bone with a piece of coral. Because coral is porous, blood vessels can grow through it.

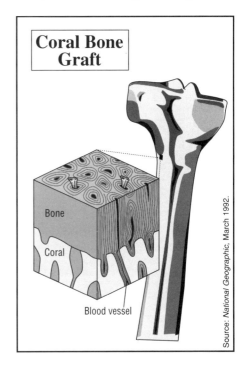

Coral Bone Graft

Bone

Coral

Blood vessel

Source: *National Geographic*, March 1992.

understand more about the human nervous system. Scientists have discovered that the triggering mechanism of a jellyfish is similar to the way human nerve synapses fire. Also, jellyfish tentacles fire poisonous barbs into victims. These barbs deaden the victim's pain receptors. At the same time, a deadly toxin poisons the numbed victim. Since the enzyme in jellyfish barbs affects nerve receptors, it may also prove useful as a local anesthetic for human beings.

Scientists are only beginning to understand how the chemicals, minerals, and enzymes in the ocean can be useful to humans. Since the ocean is three times the size of land and much more difficult to explore, scientists have done much less ocean research than they have land studies. In addition, a much greater variety of species exists in the water than on land. As a result, many scientists believe that the ocean holds the potential for many more medical breakthroughs.

Mineral resources

The ocean water is full of minerals. Salt is the most common mineral found in saltwater, but every mineral found on land—including gold—is dissolved in ocean water. Minerals make up a very small portion of ocean water, however. As a result, the cost of removing such elements from the water usually exceeds their value. One exception to this rule is magnesium chloride.

Magnesium is a light metal that is strong enough for construction. It does not occur in a pure state in nature, but does occur in combination with other elements. A chemical process is used to remove magnesium from ocean water. Since ocean water contains 0.13 percent magnesium (a high percentage for a rare element), this valuable mineral can be profitably mined from the ocean.

The ocean is a source of other products as well. Sand and gravel are removed from the ocean floor for use in construction. Limestone, which also is used for building, is found in the ocean as well as on land. Shallow tropical ar-

eas of the ocean and lagoons near coral reefs develop limestone deposits. Limestone is popular in construction because it is easily carved.

These seaside cliffs are composed of limestone, a popular material in building and construction.

Ocean energy

Any swimmer who has been knocked down by an ocean wave or dragged out to sea by a rip current knows that powerful forces reside within the ocean. For centuries, people have looked upon the ocean's power with awe. A few have tried to harness its energy for human use.

One of the first attempts to use the energy of the ocean came when people built mills beside the ocean. Like mills built on rivers and streams, ocean mills used a large paddle wheel to capture the energy of moving water. The mills were built over canals that extended into the ocean. As the ocean waves rushed toward land, water surged down the canal and into the wheelhouse. The moving water pushed against the paddles of the wheel, causing it to turn. Because the wheel was connected by a series of gears to a grindstone, when the wheel turned, so did the grindstone.

Wave-powered mills did not prove to be very efficient, however. For one thing, the movement of the water into the canal was not steady. (Waves are separated from each other by a lapse of several seconds. They are also not uniform in size. Some waves are large and powerful, others are small and weak.) The action of the tides also affected the efficiency of ocean mills. The gravitational force of the sun and the moon caused ocean waters to rise and fall twice each day. As a result, the level of water in the mill changed throughout the day, affecting the efficiency of the wheel.

Hydroelectricity

In the eighteenth century, scientists discovered that rapidly turning wheels connected to magnets could be used to generate electricity. Some force was needed to turn the wheels, however. The design for water-powered grain mills was soon adopted to create power plants. The water in streams and rivers was used to turn paddle wheels. This motion, in turn, generated electricity. Because this process of creating electricity used water, it became known as hydroelectric power.

Just as grain mills on rivers inspired the creation of mills by the ocean, so, too, did the creation of inland hydroelectric plants suggest the possibility of generating electricity from the surf. Seaside hydroelectric plants differ from those on rivers and reservoirs, however. Most ocean-powered hydroelectric plants are built with pipes that extend into the water. The pipes contain a series of turbines. As the waves move toward shore, water rushes into the pipes, causing the turbines to spin and create electricity.

Scientists today are testing new ways to generate electricity from ocean forces. Some are studying currents to see if the tremendous energy involved in their movement could be captured for human use. Another process, Ocean Thermal Energy Conversion (OTEC), uses the difference in the temperature of ocean water to generate electricity. The only by-product of the OTEC method is desalinated seawater. Before it can be implemented, though, scientists first need to be sure the process does not excessively cool or heat up any areas of the ocean.

Oil and natural gas

Someday these new technologies may tap the vast powers of the ocean. Until they do, however, the greatest storehouse of energy in the ocean resides not in its water, but below its floor in great reservoirs of oil and natural gas. Oil, or petroleum, is created when organic matter decomposes and is pressed down with excessive force and heat. The weight of ocean water has helped create petroleum deposits deep under the ocean floor. This same process creates natural gas, which collects at the top of these underground

This offshore drilling platform supports equipment that extracts oil and natural gas from beneath the ocean floor.

reserves. Oil and natural gas are removed from the ocean in the same way that they are on land. Drills cut a hole to the reserve and pipes and pumps bring the oil to the surface. Since the ocean's reserves are far from land, oil companies build offshore oil rigs, or drilling platforms anchored to the ocean floor. Most scientists believe that the amount of oil beneath the ocean far exceeds the reserves on land.

Unknown risks

Throughout human history, the ocean has proven to be a rich resource for humankind. Until this century, however, most of the ocean's riches lay beyond the grasp of people, whose explorations were limited to the ocean's surface. With the advent of submarines and other underwater technology, this barrier has been removed. People now routinely explore and exploit marine resources at greater depths than ever before.

Such forays into the deep carry risks as well as benefits. The global ocean contains many ecosystems, not all of which are fully understood. It is possible that in their pursuit of the ocean's riches, people may permanently damage or even destroy these ecosystems. Since the global ocean's ecosystem is made up of the many smaller ecosystems within it, damage to one or more of the smaller ecosystems may end up changing or even destroying the larger one. This would not bode well for humankind, since the well-being of all the creatures on the planet depends on the ongoing health of the global ocean.

Many scientists believe that despite the increased exploitation of marine resources, the global ocean remains healthy. Other scientists are not so sure. Some believe that signs of a damaged ocean have already begun to surface.

3

Harvesting the Ocean

FOR MANY PEOPLE, the term "deep-sea fishing" conjures up the image of a sportsman engaged in a thrilling battle with a large fish, such as a blue marlin. The reality of most deep-sea fishing is much less glamorous. The rising demand for ocean fish has created a fishing industry every bit as mechanized and efficient as the industrial plants onshore that process their catch. Since 1970, the number of fishing boats has doubled. Many of the ships in the modern fishing fleet use electronic devices that help them locate and catch fish. The increased size and efficiency of the world's fishing fleet has caused the fish stock to decline, leading to greater competition among fishermen. Harvesting the ocean is serious business.

Today's fishing vessels are ships called trawlers. Instead of catching fish one at a time with hooks and bait, the crews on these ships deploy huge, cone-shaped trawl nets that scoop up hordes of fish as the ships move through the water. Trawl nets are miles long and hundreds of yards wide. One design, called the midwater trawl net, is large enough to scoop up the Statue of Liberty.

Some trawl nets are now equipped with electronic sensors that keep the mouth of the net open to a specified distance. Other sensors alert the crews to the amount of fish caught in the nets. With nets of this size and sophistication, hundreds of tons of fish can be caught in one sweep.

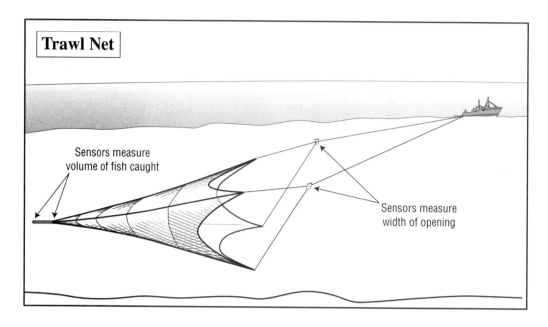

Trawl Net

Sensors measure volume of fish caught

Sensors measure width of opening

Electronic devices also help the fishing crews locate fish. Instead of relying on good weather, good luck, or an expert's knowledge of the waters, modern ships employ radar and satellite equipment to find large schools of fish. With the help of such devices, modern fishing crews are able to harvest many more fish than ever before.

Floating factories

Guided by satellites and radar, fishing vessels routinely venture far from land to pursue their catch. The distance from land creates a problem for the crews of these ships, however. They must find ways to preserve the fish until they return to land. To solve this problem, fishing crews have converted their vessels into floating factories. Not only do the crews on these vessels catch fish, they process, fillet, flash-freeze, and store them as well. Many of the larger vessels include crew quarters that have been designed to separate the living areas from processing areas. Separating the compartments helps keep morale up on long, distant voyages to open ocean waters.

Efficient as they are, these floating factories still face difficulties. The problem usually is not that the ships catch too few fish, but rather that they catch too many. In order to work efficiently, factory trawlers must process fish of similar species and sizes. With nets as large as those used, however, much more marine life is caught than can be processed. This problem exists on a scale that few land dwellers can imagine. For example, Michael Weber and Judith A. Gradwohl watched as a pair of Spanish trawlers with half-mile-broad nets stretched between them caught a massive amount of fish. The researchers noted that the crew "caught cod for their salt holds and discarded ton after ton of fish that were too small or the wrong species."

Bycatch

The fishes that fishing crews catch but do not keep are called bycatch, because they are an undesirable but unavoidable by-product of fishing. Bycatch ranges from the smallest fish in the marine food chain to dolphins, which often get caught in tuna nets. The UN Food and Agricultural Organization (FAO) in Rome estimates that 57 billion pounds of marine life caught per year worldwide is discarded as bycatch. The trauma of being trapped and hauled out of the water for sorting takes its toll on the bycatch. Most of the fish are dead or dying by the time they are thrown back.

This porpoise died in Mexico's Sea of Cortez when its tail became entangled in the ropes of a shrimp trawl net.

There are many reasons why fishing crews discard the marine life they trap in their nets. Some creatures, such as squid and manta rays, have little or no commercial value, so they become bycatch. Other fish, known as groundfish, have commercial value, but they are either not in season, too small to keep, or not processed the same way as the fish being sought. It is cheaper to discard these fish than to try to use them. The routine practice of discarding edible fish strikes some people as wasteful. Citing a 1995 bycatch report from the Alaskan fisheries, Tony Knowles, the governor of Alaska, pointed out, "Groundfish discards would have provided roughly 50 million meals."

Bycatch is not limited to fish harvesting. Shrimp fisheries are among the most wasteful fisheries in the world, according to reports from the FAO. Michael Satchell, an expert who has studied American fisheries, states:

> For every pound of shrimp hauled from the Atlantic and the Gulf of Mexico, for example, an estimated nine pounds of red snapper, croaker, mackerel, sea trout, spot, drum, and other species are brought up in the nets and tossed overboard.

Most of this shrimping bycatch has commercial value. The National Marine Fisheries Service estimates that the U.S. shrimping industry wastes more than 1 billion pounds of edible fish—an amount equal to 10 percent of the nation's annual harvest.

A void in the food chain

The loss of so many fish—catch and bycatch alike—affects the entire ocean ecosystem. Fish that are harvested and those that die beside them in the nets as bycatch leave a void in the food chain. Creatures that normally prey on these fish have less to eat. At the same time, the creatures that the harvested fish would have eaten flourish.

A disruption in the food chain can be devastating to many species. For example, if one type of fish eats sea urchins, and those fish are harvested or destroyed as bycatch, the sea urchins will not be eaten. The number of sea urchins then increases to a point at which they become pests to other sea life. The extra urchins spread out, attaching themselves to seaweed or coral. This invasion can prove deadly not only to the seaweed and coral, but also to the many marine creatures that depend on the seaweed or coral for food or protection. The loss of these creatures, in turn, will affect the plants or animals that prey on them for food. The chain reaction will continue to progress throughout the ecosystem.

The effects of overfishing and bycatch waste do not necessarily end at the water's edge. The dwindling number of fish can cause a hardship for fish-eating birds, as well. For example, when the anchovy fisheries off the coast of Peru were depleted in the 1980s, guano birds, which eat the anchovy, had to fly farther and farther from their nests to find food. Many never returned, and their young perished. A similar incident involving sand eels occurred near the Shetland Islands in the North Sea. These eels were found to be useful for fish oil as well as fish meal, so harvesting of them increased. Arctic terns, puffins, and other nesting birds feed sand eels to their young. When the eels were fished to near depletion during the late 1980s, the Shetland nesting birds failed to breed. With no offspring, the population of these birds dropped.

Managing seafood resources

In an effort to manage the resources of the sea, members of the United Nations drafted a treaty in the mid-1970s that governed fishing in the global ocean. The treaty gave each country bordering the ocean exclusive rights to harvest seafood within two hundred miles of its shores. Before the treaty, each nation's coastal waters, or Exclusive Economic Zone (EEZ), extended only twelve nautical miles from land. As a result, ships from neighboring nations could trawl the waters off a nation's coast, as long as they stayed outside the twelve-mile EEZ. Since fish move around in the water, one nation's overfishing could easily deplete another nation's offshore fish stock. By extending each nation's EEZ, the United Nations allowed each nation to better manage the fisheries off its coast.

The nations that signed the treaty suddenly found themselves responsible for nearly twenty times as much coastal water as before. The governments of many of these nations adopted new policies and passed new laws to better manage their vast new resources. European nations formed the European Union (EU) to set fishing limits. Japan and Canada also took steps to ensure future fisheries populations. In the United States, the Congress passed the Fishery Conservation and Management Act of 1976. Sponsored by Senator Warren Magnuson, this law, also known as the Magnuson Act, regulated American fisheries for the next twenty years.

The Magnuson Act protected U.S. fisheries, but the restrictions also fostered new problems. For instance, at the time Congress passed the act, the American fishing fleet was old and its equipment was outdated, compared with foreign fleets. The U.S. Congress authorized federal loans of more than $500 million to help upgrade the "rust-bucket" fleet. For the first time, a large number of American fishing vessels were equipped with electronic devices to locate catch. Not surprisingly, the better-equipped vessels caught more fish—and more bycatch. Thus, the newly protected U.S. fish stocks became victims of the newly upgraded U.S. fishing fleet.

As the number of U.S. fishing vessels increased, so did the competition between them. To better manage the harvest of fish, eight regional management councils created by the Magnuson Act set limits for the fishing harvest. The councils created fishing seasons, so various species could reproduce and grow without interference. The councils also placed limits, or quotas, on the number of each species a boat was allowed to catch. These limits were designed to leave enough adult fish to ensure reproduction and a continued level of the fish population. These quotas contained a major flaw, however. They did not address the problem of bycatch.

The activities of these American fishing vessels are regulated by a fishing council created under the Magnuson Act.

A crew member on a Massachusetts fishing boat cleans a load of shrimp caught in the Gulf of Maine. Less marketable fish caught at the same time— known as bycatch— are thrown back into the water.

The problem with quotas is that they are rarely enforced at sea. Usually, government officials monitor a fishing vessel's catch as it is unloaded at the dock. To comply with the quotas, fishing crews dump the excess fish in the sea. Anne Platt McGinn described the process in an article that appeared in *World Watch* magazine.

> Fishers therefore haul in everything they can, sort the catch, and dump the portion that doesn't make the quotas. The practice is called "hoovering" because fishers practically vacuum an area of water clean of marine life.

In 1996, the U.S. Congress reauthorized the Magnuson Act, adding new provisions to better enforce and manage modern fisheries. The 1996 act is designed to prevent overfishing by placing limits not only on the fish harvest but also on bycatch.

Regulation backlash

Managing seafood resources is a difficult task. Regulatory commissions must constantly weigh the environmental concern for preserving fish stocks with the economic need for an active fishing industry. For example, when Canada closed the Grand Banks fishery for five to ten years, more than forty thousand people were forced into unemployment.

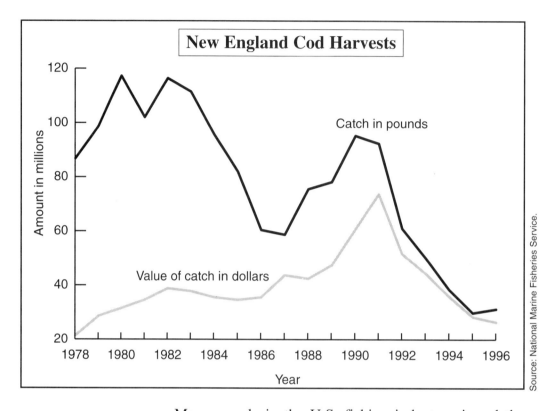

New England Cod Harvests

Amount in millions

Catch in pounds

Value of catch in dollars

Year

Source: National Marine Fisheries Service.

Many people in the U.S. fishing industry viewed the passage of the Magnuson Act and other regulations as a threat to their existence. When the New England Fishery Management Council fixed quotas on cod, haddock, yellowtail, and flounder in 1977, fishers worried that they would lose their jobs. They protested the quotas, but to no avail. Despite the quotas, the population of adult cod continued to fall. As a result, fishing crews harvested younger and smaller fish. Since the juvenile cod did not live to sexual maturity, they did not reproduce. With the birthrate of cod in decline, the council decided to close the New England cod fishery to allow the fish to recover. Despite evidence to the contrary, the fishing interests persuaded the council that they should be allowed to continue to harvest cod. According to Michael Weber and Judith Gradwohl:

> Fishermen pressed to take advantage of the profit immediately before them, and the council relented, juggling quotas and seasons so that fishermen could continue to fish these young fish down.

The council's decision led to disaster. The overfishing continued. With each new catch, the average size of the fish decreased further. Finally, the cost of locating and harvesting the cod surpassed its market value. The New England cod fishery had reached a condition known as commercial extinction. This does not mean that the species became extinct, only that its stock had been depleted to a point that made further harvesting of the fish unprofitable.

The New England fishing interests are not the only ones to harvest a fish into commercial extinction. The same thing happened to the redfish, a popular edible fish that lives in the Atlantic Ocean off the coasts of Canada, Greenland, Iceland, and Norway.

Redfish live longer than many other ocean species and they mature more slowly—an average of two or three years later than other species. As Canadian, Icelandic, and Norwegian fishermen overfished this species, the average age of their catch declined. When no redfish of mating age were left to continue the species, commercial extinction was declared. Afterward, few fishermen bothered to seek out this fish. Many marine specialists doubt if the redfish will ever recover from this disaster.

When the number of fish declines greatly, it usually becomes less profitable to harvest. This is not always the case, however. Certain types of fish are so prized that they increase in value as their numbers dwindle. Bluefin tuna, for example, brings only ten to twenty dollars per pound in New England, where the schools originate. The same fish commands as high as ninety-three dollars a pound in the Japanese market, because it is not available in local waters. As long as the value of a fish rises with its scarcity, it will remain profitable to harvest. The spiraling value of the fish means that its commercial extinction will not come much before its actual extinction.

Harvesting new species

As the stock of one type of fish dwindles, commercial fishers begin to seek new species to harvest for food. This is what happened to a fish known as pollock. Once deemed fit only for animal feed, pollock is now "processed into fish sticks and fast food," according to *National Geographic* magazine.

Marine biologists warn that new stocks of fish should be examined before they are utilized. They point to orange roughy as an example of what they mean. Orange roughy first was commercially harvested in the 1970s. At that time it was considered to be similar to most other game fish. Marine scientists now believe, however, that the popular fish has a life span that exceeds that of human beings. If this is true, it suggests that orange roughy matures very slowly. It may take decades to replenish the catch that was harvested since the 1970s. Some scientists fear that orange roughy may meet the same fate as redfish and never recover from the commercial fishing that has occurred.

Competing for fisheries

The increased regulation of the fishing industry worldwide allows nations to better manage their resources, but even strict laws can be broken. Canada learned this lesson after the government closed the Grand Banks fishery to allow for its recovery. Canadians complied with the order,

Fishermen unload their catch at a wharf in San Francisco. Fishing quotas usually are enforced on land, not at sea.

but fishing vessels from other nations did not. Canada had to take up arms against foreign trawlers poaching in the fishery's waters.

Poaching is even more common in the waters of less developed nations. Nine-tenths of the world's coastal waters belong to developing nations. The fishing fleets of these developing nations often consist of small boats capable of traveling only several miles from shore. The fishing fleets in these nations generally use only a small percentage of the nation's total waters. Fishermen in Indonesia, for example, catch almost 75 percent of their catch in only 30 percent of the nation's EEZ.

Foreign fishing fleets eye these unused waters with interest, because they are much more accessible than the international waters farther out to sea. Sometimes foreign trawlers apply for licenses to fish in the waters of the developing nations. Because these poorer countries need the money, they often sell rights that end up hurting their own people. When the nations refuse to grant such licenses, some foreign trawlers simply poach the waters, believing that the developing nation does not have the resources to enforce its own rights. The foreign trawlers sweep through the developing nation's waters, harvesting most of the desirable fish. Sometimes the trawling nets scrape against the ocean bottom, destroying the habitat of many commercial fish species. What is left for the natives are the trash fish—rejected by the foreign trawlers as worthless.

Rights granted, rights revoked

India was one of the nations that granted foreign vessels the right to fish within its maritime zone. According to these licenses, the high-tech foreign vessels were exempt from paying taxes. They also were allowed to export 80 percent of their catch. India's traditional fishermen were not pleased with the arrangement. They demanded that the government revoke all such licenses. "The enormous capacity of these ships, they claimed, threatened the livelihood of more than eight million traditional fishermen," reported Madhusree Mukerjee in a 1996 article for *Scientific American.*

The protest gathered strength when Harekrishna Debnath of the National Fishworkers' Forum (NFF) in India reported that foreign vessels were transferring their catch to other vessels in midsea, thereby hiding their catch and avoiding some of the restrictions placed on them by the Indian government. The protest resulted in all joint-venture licenses being canceled. This extreme solution does not guarantee that India's fishing problems are over. The nation must now find a way to enforce its ban on foreign trawlers.

Net loss

Banning fishing by refusing licenses, as India has, or by declaring a fishery off limits, as Canada has, are the most extreme steps governments have taken to better manage the world's marine resources. Other regulations have produced fewer headlines, but they may have had an even greater impact on the world's fisheries. These regulations have not prevented fishing. Rather, they have changed the way in which fish are caught. Regulations of this type often are easier to enact and enforce than those which prevent fishermen from earning income.

One such worldwide regulation was adopted in 1994. It banned fishing nets with openings smaller than a certain size. Nets with larger openings allowed small fish—usually juveniles of a species—to swim through the nets and avoid capture. This law helped young fish to live long enough to multiply, increasing the population of the species.

Another important regulation has curtailed the use of gill nets, which are also known as drift nets. Gill nets are made of a lightweight but strong nylon and are often many miles long. They are set out in the ocean and collected at a later time. This is similar to placing crab and lobster pots.

There are two major problems with the use of gill nets. First, they capture any and all of the marine life that crosses their path, whether it is sought by the fishermen or not. Often the fish and other sea life trapped in the nets die before they are harvested. In the warmth of tropical waters, fish caught in gill nets often rot before the nets are emp-

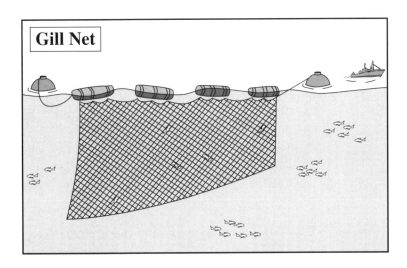

Gill Net

tied. Second, the nets often snag on the ocean bottom or break free in the ocean tides and become drifting "ghost nets." Lost at sea, they continue to trap sea life as they drift about. When this happens, the gill nets form a "wall of death," drifting through the water and killing all types of sea life from which no human will ever benefit.

Gill nets were banned in California in 1990. The United Nations declared a moratorium on their use in the open ocean in 1992. Eventually, many countries, including Japan and China, grudgingly agreed with the action.

International cooperation on issues such as the use of gill nets offers a sign of hope that solutions can be found before the world's fisheries are ruined. At the same time, the ghostly walls of death already adrift in the ocean are grim reminders of another problem that threatens the ecosystem of the global ocean: pollution.

4

Polluting the Ocean

GILL NETS ARE the largest human-made items drifting in the ocean and spreading death, but they are not the only ones. Each day, human beings release garbage, debris, chemicals, and other pollutants into the global ocean. Some of this pollution is intentional; some of it is accidental. All of it can kill.

The most visible form of pollution is garbage and debris. Plastic bottles and bottle caps, six-pack rings, trash bags, food wrappers, cigarette butts, polystyrene cups, and glass containers litter the ocean. Few of these items are biodegradable, that is, they do not decompose naturally in the environment. Instead, they stay intact, floating on the ocean's currents for decades. Drifting ocean trash has turned up almost everywhere. In 1991, for example, cleanup crews found 950 pieces of trash on the shores of Dulcie Atoll in the Pacific Ocean. Dulcie Atoll is three thousand miles from any other shore.

Dumping at sea

A great deal of ocean trash comes from boats and ships. Each day, millions of fishing boats, naval vessels, cargo ships, cruise ships, and pleasure craft take to the global ocean. Some of these ships are floating towns, bearing thousands of people. All people generate waste, so it is hardly surprising that much of the refuse from ships ends up in the sea.

Naval vessels face an especially severe challenge in waste management because their crews are so large and they spend long periods of time at sea. Tons of garbage can build up aboard each ship. To limit the amount of space needed to house garbage, the U.S. Navy is testing a machine that sanitizes and compresses plastic waste. The plastic disks created by the machine are approximately two feet in diameter and several inches thick. One day's plastic garbage can be compressed into just five or six disks. The Navy plans to have all its ships equipped with the machine by 1999.

For centuries, most mariners simply dumped their waste into the ocean. The dumping of plastics and untreated waste is no longer allowed under international law, but many of the ocean-faring crews ignore these laws. They continue to dump their trash in the ocean. Few of these lawbreakers are ever caught.

The outcome of such dumping turns up on the world's beaches each day. In recent years, conservation groups have carefully recorded the items that wash up on shore to determine the most common types of garbage entering the ocean. One of the first groups to sponsor such a program

This American coot was strangled by plastic rings discarded into the ocean.

was the Center for Marine Conservation in Texas. In 1988, the center established an annual beach cleanup program on the Texas shores. Participants recorded each item they picked up on index cards to be entered into a database. The program spread to other beaches in the United States and other countries.

The findings of such cleanup efforts were shocking. Beach cleanups, known as beach sweeps, reported 1,439 tons of garbage and debris bagged in twenty participating countries in 1992. Plastic products made up 60 percent of the total debris. Glass, metal, and paper each accounted for about 10 percent of the total. Wood, rubber, and cloth items each accounted for less than 5 percent of the total.

Since plastics do not deteriorate in water as many other types of garbage do, they pose a special threat to sea animals. Sea turtles and birds have been found strangled with plastic beverage rings around their neck. Some seals, whose snouts become entangled with plastic rings, have suffocated. Others ensnared by plastic have starved to death. Some sea animals mistake plastic debris for food; for example, turtles have died after eating floating plastic wrappers that appear to them as jellyfish. Autopsies performed on beached sea mammals have revealed that some of them have eaten plastic debris as well. Styrofoam pellets eaten by birds or other sea animals cause starvation, because the creatures feel too "full" to eat the nutritional food they need.

Ocean dumping laws

Many nations have passed laws to end ocean dumping. In the United States, for example, people who dump trash in the ocean can face fines up to fifty thousand dollars and possible imprisonment if they are convicted. MARPOL, the International Convention for the Prevention of Marine Pollution, has outlawed the dumping of plastic items into any of the world's waterways. MARPOL also strictly limits the dumping of other types of garbage. Under MARPOL regulations, nothing can be dumped within three miles of shore. Some items—including paper, glass, food, rags, and crockery—are legal to dump in a zone from three to twelve miles offshore, provided the items have been ground into pieces of less than an inch in diameter. Items that have not been ground into small pieces must be hauled at least twelve miles from shore before they are dumped.

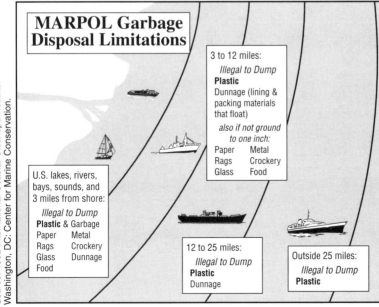

Source: *1992 International Coastal Cleanups Results.* Washington, DC: Center for Marine Conservation.

MARPOL Garbage Disposal Limitations

3 to 12 miles:
Illegal to Dump
Plastic
Dunnage (lining & packing materials that float)

also if not ground to one inch:
Paper   Metal
Rags   Crockery
Glass   Food

U.S. lakes, rivers, bays, sounds, and 3 miles from shore:
Illegal to Dump
Plastic & Garbage
Paper   Metal
Rags   Crockery
Glass   Dunnage
Food

12 to 25 miles:
Illegal to Dump
Plastic
Dunnage

Outside 25 miles:
Illegal to Dump
Plastic

Sewage

As long as human beings have lived near the ocean not only their trash, but also their bodily waste has found its way into the water. As people build villages, towns, and cities by the sea, the problem increases. Martha Gorman in her book *Environmental Hazards: Marine Pollution* states:

> As permanent, settled communities replaced nomadic tribes, less human and animal waste was returned to the land and more was concentrated in the nearest body of water, either as runoff or sewage.

Today both treated and untreated sewage is pumped into the ocean every day. Modern sewage treatment plants in New England alone discharge 575 billion gallons of contaminated water into the ocean each year, according to a 1992 *CQ Researcher* article. In addition, the article's author, Rodman D. Griffin, reported, "another 700 billion gallons of polluted storm water flows annually into the sea from the region's urban areas."

Because sewage is organic in nature, the ocean is capable of breaking it down. Unfortunately, the process of doing so can upset the balance of the ocean ecosystem.

Eutrophication

Sewage is rich in phosphorus and nitrogen. When sewage is dumped into the ocean, the algae, fungi, and bacteria that live in the water feast on these nutrients. This process helps break the sewage down. However, the organisms feeding on the sewage also consume oxygen. Since sewage is rich in nutrients, the organisms multiply quickly, consuming more and more of the oxygen in the water. This process is called eutrophication. As a result, the growing colonies of organisms can drain the oxygen out of nearby waters, creating what scientists refer to as biological oxygen demand (BOD). Martha Gorman concludes, "If there is too little oxygen in the water to sustain these biodegraders, they die and so do all the plants and animals that depend on them."

Bays are especially prone to eutrophication. People used to think that currents carried the waste out of bays and into the sea, but scientists now know this is not the case. Bays and harbors have relatively low water circulation. As a result, most sewage waste settles on the bottom, where algae, fungi, and bacteria consume it. Because bay water does not circulate very much, the sewage-eating organisms can deplete the oxygen levels in it quickly.

Chesapeake Bay, on the Atlantic coast of the United States, was on the path to eutrophication before the U.S. government and the local governments of five states surrounding the bay took action. The federal and state governments worked together to limit the amount of sewage entering the bay. As a result of these programs, phosphorus levels have dropped 75 percent since 1981. In addition, 10 million dollars has been spent to find ways to reduce nitrogen levels.

Further problems, possible solutions

Eutrophication is not the only problem the breakdown of sewage causes. Some of the organisms that feed off the sewage, such as bacteria, can cause disease when consumed by other creatures in the food chain. For example, crustaceans, such as oysters and clams, can absorb bacteria that are harmful to humans. People who consume contaminated clams and oysters may get sick or even die.

Since most sewage is deliberately released into the ocean, it is one of the simplest sources of pollution to control. In 1992, MARPOL banned the release of sewage into the ocean from either ships or pleasure boats. At the same time, governments around the world are regulating sewage treatment more closely. Some treatment plants now triple-process sewage, separating the solids from liquid waste and processing each separately. Solids are disposed of in landfills or processed into fertilizer or mulch. The liquid waste is discharged into the ocean beyond the confines of bays and harbors for better dilution in open ocean waters.

Oil and water

Sewage waste will break down rather quickly in ocean water, but this is not the case with another pollutant with organic origins—oil. Although it is formed from decomposed plant and animal life, oil does not dilute in water very easily. Instead, it floats on the surface. In large amounts, it can block sunlight to the plants and animals below the surface. When oil comes in contact with animals, it can coat the surface of their bodies with a sticky film that can irritate and even suffocate them.

Nearly half of the oil in the ocean water comes from the routine operation of marine vessels. Each day, oil used to lubricate engines and to power the vessels leaks into the ocean. In addition, the crews of cargo ships routinely flush out their holding tanks and rinse residue off their decks. Any oil that is present washes into the sea.

Another source of oil pollution comes from accidents at sea. Much of the world's oil is transported from one country to another across the ocean in huge tankers. The movement of so much oil on the world's waterways presents a huge danger to the environment. A single mishap involving an oil tanker can cause tremendous damage to the ocean ecosystem. The world was reminded of the destructive power of oil when a ship named the *Exxon Valdez* ran aground in Prince William Sound, off Alaska, in 1989. The giant tanker spilled 11 million gallons of crude oil into Prince William Sound. Slowly the oil drifted into the Gulf of Alaska. Within a week, the spill had fouled one thousand miles of shoreline.

Not all oil is the same. None of it is good for the environment, but some kinds are worse than others. Light, refined oils, such as kerosene, evaporate quickly. When kerosene is spilled into water, it is relatively easy to clean up. Heavier oils, such as fuel oil, remain on the surface longer than kerosene does. Crude oil is the worst. It forms a thick slick on the water and leaves a sticky residue on anything that gets in its way—rocks, animals, birds, or human beings. Unfortunately for the ocean ecosystem, the *Exxon Valdez* was carrying crude oil.

These otters died after being coated with crude oil spilled by the Exxon Valdez.

Cleanup crews used booms to contain the spill then covered the water with other absorbent material to soak up the oil. Despite their efforts, at least 33,000 sea birds, 146 eagles, and 980 sea otters were killed by the viscous oil from the *Exxon Valdez*. Cleanup crews continued working for six months to clean up the spill. They scoured the beaches with a high-pressure spray of hot water, a technique that worked well but ended up killing some fish in the surface waters. Five years after the spill, oil was still resurfacing from beneath rocks and pebbles along the shoreline.

The *Exxon Valdez* spill was the largest spill in 1989, but it was not the only one. Several months earlier, an Argentine ship capsized off the Antarctic Peninsula. In June, three separate spills occurred within twelve hours of each other, off the coast of Rhode Island, in the Delaware River, and in Galveston Bay. After the "year of the oil spill," oil companies were pressed to take responsibility. They started using double-walled oil compartments so that damage could occur to the ship's outer hull without necessarily puncturing the holding tanks.

An international spill

Most oil spills are accidents, but a few are deliberate. During the Gulf War, for example, the leader of Iraq, Saddam

Hussein, ordered his troops to dump oil into the Persian Gulf as they retreated from Kuwait. The Iraqi army dumped an estimated 4 to 12 million barrels of Kuwaiti oil into the Persian Gulf. Hussein also ordered the Kuwaiti oil fields burned. The smoke from the burning oil not only fouled the air, but much of it also ended up settling on the waters of the Persian Gulf. The equivalent of 4 to 5 million barrels of oil was deposited in the ocean by the oil-laden smoke. The nation of Saudi Arabia was most affected by this intentional dumping. According to Michael Weber and Judith Grad-wohl: "The counterclockwise currents of the Persian Gulf carried much of the oil released during the Gulf War south until it reached the Abu Ali peninsula, which confined the slick against the Saudi coast." There the oil polluted the shore and killed sea mammals, birds, and other wildlife.

Chemical pollution

Oil is probably the best-known pollutant of ocean water, but it is not the only one. Many different chemicals wash into the ocean each day from a variety of sources. Some of these chemicals, such as benzene, lead, and mercury, come from the wastewater of industrial plants. Other chemicals, such as chlorofluorocarbons, billow from factory smoke-stacks, drift over the water, and settle into the ocean from the air. Still other chemicals, such as pesticides and fertil-izers used in agriculture, reach the ocean by washing into rivers and streams that flow into the sea.

Once the chemical pollutants reach the sea, they can irri-tate any creatures that come in contact with them. Rashes and lesions have been found on the skin of fish, dolphins, and even some people who swim in polluted waters. Even worse, harmful chemicals can be absorbed by many types of marine life and enter into the food chain. As larger ani-mals consume the smaller animals, they ingest larger and larger amounts of the chemical pollutants. Some chemicals, such as mercury, can cause tissue damage and birth defects in the species that consume them—including humans.

Unlike the organic pollutants discharged by sewage plants, chemical pollutants do not break down easily. As a result, they can remain lethal for years. The pesticide DDT, for example, continues to pollute ocean waters more than twenty-five years after it was banned in the United States and many other nations. Traces of DDT have turned up in Antarctic penguins and arctic marine life, thousands of miles from the lands where the pesticide was used.

Another group of compounds that remain in the ocean habitat long after they were banned are polychlorinated biphenyls, or PCBs. Banned worldwide in 1979, these compounds once were used in insulation and in the manufacturing process. They reached the ocean primarily through factory runoff. Because they were made from petroleum, PCBs did not dissolve in water. Absorbed by plants and tiny marine life, PCBs worked their way through the food chain until they were consumed by fish, marine mammals, and seabirds. Trace amounts of PCBs were passed through the eggs of six generations of some marine birds.

Marine biologist Roger Payne believes that PCB build-up breaks down the immune systems of some sea animals, making them more susceptible to disease. "The oceans may be suffering from a condition similar to AIDS," Payne states, referring to the disease caused by a virus that breaks down the human immune system.

Manufactured chemicals such as DDT and PCBs are not the only substances that are toxic to marine life. Some organic compounds pose dangers to the global ecosystem as well. When masses of fish began to die off in the Gulf of Bothnia, which separates Sweden from Finland, scientists suspected that human-made chemicals were to blame. Knowing paper mills often use chlorinated chemicals known as dioxins to process wood pulp, researchers suspected that the region's paper mills were poisoning the fish. The researchers were only partly right. Most of the harm was being caused by kraft pulping mills. (Kraft pulping is a method of paper making

A helicopter sprays pesticide onto a field. Rain often washes pesticides from farmlands and into waterways that empty into the ocean.

that does not use human-made chemicals.) A natural compound found in the wood was toxic to the fish.

Ocean accumulation

Chemical pollutants do not have to be absorbed directly to threaten marine life. Sometimes the mere presence of some chemicals can disturb the delicate balance in the ocean ecosystem. For example, thin slicks of oil, detergents, and sediments that float on the water can keep sunlight from reaching plants on the coastal floor. Without sunlight, these plants cannot convert carbon dioxide into oxygen. This can lead to biological oxygen demand and even eutrophication. Without sufficient sunlight, many plants die, and a vital source of food for many marine creatures disappears. Because juvenile marine life tends to live in shallow coastal water, they often are affected most by surface pollution. As in the case of overfishing, when juveniles of a certain species disappear, a link in the food chain is broken, and many other species can be affected.

Sources of pollution

Chemical pollution is more difficult to control than sewage pollution. There are many reasons for this. Unlike sewage, which often is pumped directly into the ocean through a large pipe, the sources of chemical pollutants are not always obvious. "One-third of pollutants entering the marine environment come from air emissions, a large portion of which settle into coastal waters," reports Peter Weber, a research associate for the Worldwatch Institute, an environmental research organization. Other pollutants enter the ocean as runoff from the land. Road oil, detergents, and other chemicals are washed into storm drains, creeks, streams, and rivers by rain and snow. Because this pollution does not enter the ecosystem at specific points, it is known as nonpoint pollution. Because nonpoint pollution can originate many miles from the ocean, it is virtually impossible to trace its source.

Another major source of chemical pollution comes from coastal dredgings—mud and silt that are removed from the

Smoke can drift for many miles before finally settling on ocean water. Such pollution, referred to as nonpoint, is very difficult to trace to its source.

floor of bays, harbors, and other coastal areas to widen or deepen channels for shipping traffic. According to World-watch research associate Peter Weber, 80 to 90 percent of all the materials dumped at sea are dredgings. Although consisting primarily of organic material, dredgings are rich in toxic chemicals that have accumulated over a period of many years. Weber estimates that 10 percent of dredgings are contaminated with toxic chemicals. Most of the pollutants in dredgings come from nonpoint sources, so their origins are impossible to trace.

Without proof that specific companies are to blame for ocean pollution, few industry leaders will bother to change their practices. Many companies responsible for polluting the ocean are located so far from the ocean that their executives sincerely doubt that their operations have any impact on the ocean ecosystem. Furthermore, antipollution measures can be very costly to adopt. To reduce pollution, some companies would have to revamp their entire manufacturing process, an expense that could put the cost of the companies' products beyond the reach of average consumers. If people cannot afford a company's products, they will not buy them, and the company will go out of business. No business will commit economic suicide out of a vague desire to help the environment. That is why many governments around the world have adopted strict laws against releasing chemicals directly into the air, into the waterways, or even onto the land.

Deep ocean dumping

To prevent companies from dumping toxic chemicals into the air, water, and soil, governments often require them to dispose of dangerous materials in a certain way. One widely used pollutant disposal method is to seal the chemicals into containers and dump them somewhere where it is believed they will do no harm. That place is often the deep waters of the ocean.

Many experts believe that the dumping of containers of chemicals into the ocean poses its own threat to the environment. For proof, some of these experts point to a two-square-mile expanse located eighteen miles off the eastern coast of the United States. The official name of this area is the Massachusetts Bay Industrial Waste Site, but locals refer to it simply as the Foul Area. From 1953 to 1976, this area served as a dumping ground for sealed containers of toxic and radioactive materials. A video survey of the site, taken during the summer of 1991, showed almost one hundred objects scattering the ocean floor at eighteen separate sites. Joseph Raulinaitis, public affairs specialist for the FDA's

"I like to recreate their natural environment."

Boston office, reports: "Sixty-four of the objects were identified as cement containers used to dispose of dangerous materials, and more than half of them had broken open."

In a joint effort between several state and federal agencies, seafood from these areas and the surrounding waters was collected and tested for dangerous levels of hazardous or toxic chemicals. Though test results indicated trace contaminants in seafood, none had levels high enough to pose threats, according to the Food and Drug Administration.

At one location, however, when a research vessel's anchor was pulled aboard, the tip had traces of radioactive waste high enough to set off the sensors worn by the crew. The participants of the study were also surprised to find that, despite posted warnings, fishermen routinely harvested fish from waters directly above the dump sites.

The United States is just one of many nations to use the ocean as a dumping ground. After World War II thousands of tons of munitions were dumped in the waters off Germany, Denmark, Norway, Sweden, and Poland. The former Soviet Union dumped large amounts of radioactive waste into the Barents and Kara Seas.

Because a majority of chemical pollutants come from land-based sources or from nonpoint pollution, it is difficult to place blame with a particular industry or source. The United States has prompted an international conference to address this threat to the marine environment. The governments belonging to the United Nations have agreed to focus efforts on stopping and cleaning up nonpoint pollution. Plans are being discussed for effective ways to target and enforce this source of pollution. Limiting the percentage of air emissions and revamping wastewater treatment are some suggested ways to cut down on nonpoint pollution. How to enforce these methods is still in question.

Species pollution

Garbage, sewage, oil, chemicals, and radioactive waste—these human-made products make up a witch's brew of pollution that threatens the global ocean. Not all ocean pollutants originate on land, however. Some of the most destructive pollutants are quite at home in the ocean: they are living plants and animals that invade habitats where they have never lived, and where they have no natural enemies. In these conditions, alien species can multiply wildly, consuming precious resources and destroying the balance of an ecosystem.

Although they do not manufacture these rampant species, human beings are responsible for their introduction into new habitats. It is people who move these creatures from their natural homes and deposit them in places where they do not belong. This usually happens when cargo ships take on seawater for ballast. This water often contains marine life. Trapped inside the ships, the marine life remains sometimes for months until it is released in distant waters. Often, the marine life cannot survive in the new ecosystem, but sometimes it thrives.

Disrupting the ecosystem

For example, when a Japanese vessel discharged ballast water containing red algae into Australian waters, the alien species bloomed out of control. The growth of the red algae caused not only red tides, but also high concentrations of the algae in shallow waters along the shore. A gulp of seawater or a bite of shellfish contaminated by the red algae can make an animal or a person violently ill.

When a species has no natural predators in an environment, its growth can be astonishing. A few years after they were accidentally released into the waters of the Great Lakes of the United States, zebra mussels numbered in the millions. Huge colonies of the tiny crustacean could be found clinging to rocks, boats, pipes, and anything else in the water. The mussels became a nuisance, clogging drainage pipes and causing wastewater to back up. They got inside underwater machinery and caused it to malfunction. The problem was so bad that the National Guard was called in to try to clean up the mess.

The zebra mussel was not the first exotic species to enter the Great Lakes in ballast water, but the U.S. Coast Guard hopes it will be the last. U.S. law now requires all ocean

Zebra mussels cling to the rudder of a ship. A species that is alien to the Great Lakes of the United States, the zebra mussel has multiplied into the millions.

vessels to discharge ballast water before entering the St. Lawrence Seaway, the waterway that connects the Great Lakes to the Atlantic Ocean. International regulations also prohibit the release of ballast water in harbors. The crews of oceangoing vessels are advised to take on ballast water in the open ocean where the chance of picking up exotic species is greatly reduced.

The problem of alien species serves as a reminder of how delicately the ecosystems of the global ocean are balanced. One small change—the introduction of even one new species—can upset an entire ecosystem. This is especially true along the coastlines of the global ocean, where the majority of marine life is located. Unfortunately, the coastlines are also the part of the ocean most affected by human activities. Not surprisingly, the coastal zones are a major battleground in the fight to save the ocean habitat.

5

The Coastal Zone

THE COASTAL AREAS of the world are among the most fertile on Earth. Often called the coastal zone, this area begins at the coastal plain—a broad, level expanse of land along the seacoast that gently slopes toward the ocean—and extends to the end of the continental shelf, the gently sloping land that is submerged in water. This submerged shelf can reach a depth of about six hundred feet before the ocean bottom drops off steeply into the deep ocean.

The coastal zone includes 8 percent of the world's surface. Comprising a variety of habitats, this 8 percent of the earth is home to 25 percent of the world's human population and 90 percent of all marine life. In the United States, for example, half the population lives within fifty miles of coastlines on the Atlantic, the Pacific, the Gulf of Mexico, and the Great Lakes.

Soil in the coastal zone is rich in minerals, whether above or below the water. Major farming areas are located near the coast where fertile soil is the product of an ocean that retreated millions of years ago. This same rich soil makes up the ocean floor. Most of the ocean's plant life grows in the shallower waters of the continental shelf. This plant life accounts for 26 percent of the total plant productivity on Earth. According to Libby Smith, technical writer and editor for New York State's Department of Environmental Conservation, in her 1990 article for the *Conservationist*:

> For centuries people have assumed that the ocean is so vast that it can absorb all of our wastes without ill effect. Now we recognize that this is not so. The damage we have inflicted is especially evident at the ocean's edges—the beaches, harbors, marshes and inlets.

Ocean life

The ocean's continental shelf is teeming with marine life. From the smallest plants, which are called phytoplankton, to algae, zooplankton, fish, crustaceans, sponges, and seaweed, the shallower ocean waters provide the proper balance of sunlight, oxygen, and minerals for marine life to thrive. Many sea plants and animals live on the ocean bottom. Most, such as kelp, coral, and sponges are fixed to the ocean floor and remain there for their entire lives.

Phytoplankton and other food is carried to them by the currents. Because sunlight is important for their growth, most sea plants cannot live deeper than the sun's rays reach. And many forms of sea life that utilize these plants for food or protection are bound to live within that environment. These compact ecosystems are easily disturbed by changes in the coastal waters.

Coral reefs

Coral reefs are an example of a delicate marine species that is also an ecosystem of its own. Worldwatch research associate Peter Weber reports in a 1994 article:

An oil-soaked shoreline. Ocean pollution is most evident in coastal areas.

The unique ecology of the coral reefs make them one of the world's most diverse ecosystems, second in density of unique species only to tropical rain forests, thus the widespread damage to these reefs constitutes a major blow to the Earth's overall biological diversity.

Lining sixty thousand miles (one hundred thousand kilometers) of coast, they harbor numerous species of marine plant and animal life. Fish that hide among the coral shelves include the variety of colorful tropical fish sold for aquariums, larger fish such as grouper and wrasse, parrot fish, which nibble algae and bite off bits of the coral, small varieties of shark, octopuses, sea urchins, and several types of algae.

The coral itself is actually a living organism, not a dead shell or skeleton as once thought. Though it is an animal, it relies on the sunlight as plants do for survival. Coral works as a team with zooxanthellae, an algae that lives in its translucent tissues. These algae supply the coral with food and oxygen in return for a safe place to live. Fish deposit their eggs in coral for protection and many juvenile fish seek shelter among the reefs' wide-spreading, shelflike layers.

The Great Barrier Reef off the northeastern coast of Australia. Coral reefs are home to countless species of marine life.

Coral reefs are among the most productive fisheries on the planet. They hold one-tenth of all fish caught. For developing countries they supply as much as 25 percent of their total marine catch. According to Weber:

> Reefs are saltwater supermarkets of food and raw materials, especially for traditional coastal and island people. Pacific islanders receive up to 90 percent of their animal protein from reef fish, and people in Southeast Asia, the Caribbean, and parts of South Asia and East Africa derive a significant portion of the protein in their diets from the fish that live in these ecosystems.

The wealth of coral reefs may be their demise, because the fish and other marine life attract the only known enemy of coral: people. Fishermen routinely drag their nets through the reefs, throwing the ecosystem out of balance and damaging the coral itself. Fishers of exotic species such as wrasse and grouper, which are delicacies in Hong Kong, wreak havoc of a different sort on the reefs. For the Chinese, the ability to afford these exotic fish is a sign of one's economic status, so customers are willing to pay very high prices for them. Patrons of fancy restaurants require, however, that the fish be alive so they can select their fish from the restaurant aquariums. Because the fish must be delivered alive, fishermen catch them by stunning them and then scooping them out of the water. To quickly stun the fish in a reef, fishermen squirt cyanide into the water or detonate small explosives in the area. Both methods shock the fish, which float to the surface of the water; they are then captured and revived in a holding tank. Both methods damage the delicate polyps of the reefs and poison the surrounding waters.

The "stun and revive" method is also used to capture the small, bright, tropical fish that many people keep in home aquariums. Most people would not think that having an aquarium as a hobby was hurting the ocean environment in any way. The method used to capture fish for aquariums, however, damages reefs, poisons the surrounding waters, and ultimately alters the coastline when these habitats are destroyed. It can take a coral reef years to recover from the shock or damage inflicted by fishermen.

Understanding the danger to the reefs, many governments have taken steps to protect them. Such sanctuaries have become major tourist attractions. Thousands of scuba divers and skin divers descend into coral reefs each year. Sometimes, however, visitors to the "protected" reefs break off pieces of coral for souvenirs, walk on the reefs, or even scribble graffiti on them. As the polyps and zooxanthellae die, the organisms that depend on these parts of the coral reef also die. A coral reef specialist working at the Australian Institute of Marine Science estimates that "fully 10 percent of the world's reefs have been degraded beyond recognition. Another 30 percent are in critical condition and will be lost completely in 10 to 20 years."

Natural buffer zones

Many coral reefs function as natural seawalls, reducing the erosive action of the ocean by absorbing the impact of the waves. At the same time, areas along the coastline not only provide a buffer between the ocean and the land, but also keep shore sediments from washing onto and suffocating the coral reefs. In these areas, called coastal or estuarine wetlands, freshwater washes toward the ocean and mixes with the salty water flowing toward shore. These brackish waters serve as spawning and nursery grounds for much of the ocean's plant and animal life. They also provide protection and nesting areas for many types of waterfowl and land animals and birds.

Wetlands include all the areas where rivers or tributaries meet larger bodies of water. Depending upon the amount of land they include, they may be called marshes, swamps, deltas, or estuaries. They are often part of the watershed area for bays and harbors. Wetlands serve as natural buffer zones between the ocean and land. Coarse grasses and reeds with strong roots hold the plants upright when sea surges flood the wetlands. The root system traps pollution and sediments flowing from inland streams. Wetlands are distinct ecosystems that serve not only marine life, but also a variety of land plants, birds, and animals, which depend on these habitats for food and shelter.

Once considered waste-lands, swamps and other coastal wetlands provide protection and food for many plants and animals.

Uninhabitable and without obvious signs of wealth, wetlands have been traditionally regarded as wasteland—something to be improved if it is to have value. For generations, people have drained and filled in coastal marshes, swamps, and bogs in order to make usable property. According to Michael Satchell, a staff reporter for *U.S. News & World Report,* the state of Louisiana "loses about 50 square miles of piscatorial [fish] breeding grounds annually" to coastal development. Not only are fish affected. The destruction of wetlands also affects the breeding of insects, waterfowl, reptiles, sea otters, and many other creatures. Many of these species, such as reptiles and waterfowl, are on the endangered species list because of the destruction of their habitats.

Rivers and streams are also affected by coastal development. Waterways that feed estuaries are often rerouted so the swamps and wetlands will dry up, allowing loggers to harvest timber. Some rivers and streams are dammed to permit fish farming. Such improvements can be costly to the environment and to the pocketbooks of taxpayers. For example, Steve Kemper reported in a 1992 *Smithsonian* article on coastal development:

Florida's Kissimmee River meanders toward the canal built by the Corps of Engineers. Straightening the course of the river harmed the ecosystem that had developed in the river's basin.

Thirty years ago the Corps of Engineers spent ten years and $32 million to turn Florida's flood-prone, serpentine Kissimmee River into a neat canal. That led to suffocation of the ecosystem in the surrounding 75 square mile river basin. Now the Corps intends to put the kinks back into the river, at a cost of $370 million over 15 years.

Americans are not the only ones to learn about the high cost of tampering with wetlands. The Dutch also have learned this lesson. For centuries, the Dutch have used dams and dikes to reroute their waterways and create nutrient-rich farmland. Despite the fact that the country had ample farmland, the Dutch government has continued to convert wetlands into farming land. "Draining wetlands has reduced the natural habitat for wildlife and driven the Dutch national symbol, the stork, from the country," notes Peter Weber. Although the Dutch still plan to use dams and dikes to control the huge watershed making up most of their country, they also plan to restore some of the areas to their original wetlands state.

Mangrove forests

Found in a wide tropical belt along the coasts of south and southeastern Asia, South America, and Africa, mangrove forests are another unique coastal habitat. By trapping soils that would end up washing into coastal waters and onto reefs, mangrove forests create a nutrient-rich environment for over two thousand species of fish, shellfish, crested worms, and other marine life.

The root system of the mangrove trees provides footing for sponges. Their canopies provide sanctuary for hundreds of species of birds. Marine mammals, such as manatees and otters, also seek refuge in mangrove forests. Like coral reefs, mangrove forests absorb the impact of storm waves rolling toward shore, and they provide breeding grounds and shelter for juvenile fish and other marine species.

Mangrove forests are a great source of timber; therefore they often are cleared by loggers. Sometimes the forests are cut down to make way for commercial and residential uses. In Ecuador, many mangrove forests have been cleared to create shrimp ponds. As a result, in these areas, the mangrove forests no longer protect the nearby coral reefs from silt and sand.

Not only do the mangrove forests prevent silt from fouling the coral reefs offshore, but they also trap dangerous pollutants before they enter the ocean water. In fact, all wetlands serve as a kind of filter, helping to keep pollutants that flow into them from rivers and streams from draining into the sea. When coastal forests and wetlands are destroyed, this natural pollution buffer is also destroyed. Without the protection of the wetlands, juvenile fish and other marine plants and animals struggle to survive.

Erosion

The incredible vistas enjoyed by people living within sight of the ocean make owning seafront property highly desirable. To provide more buildable land, wetlands are filled in, sand dunes are leveled, and the entire coastline is reshaped. According to Don Hinrichsen, environmental analyst:

> Along the Kenyan coast, from Mombasa north to Malindi, sleepy fishing villages have been replaced with tourist hotels and resorts, a process that has profoundly affected coastal ecosystems. With mangroves removed wholesale and reefs used for building material, coastal erosion is now an imminent threat to the entire region.

To provide protection to beachfront property, builders put in jetties, breakwaters, and groins. These human "improvements" over nature's buffer zones have recently been found to increase the erosion of coastlines, according to coastal geologists.

Along a natural seacoast, ocean currents push sand down the coast. This constant movement of sand replenishes the beaches. If the path of the sand is blocked by a jetty, or stone wall built into the water, the movement of the sand is interrupted. Most jetties are built to keep sand from filling in a dredged-out channel. The jetty can accomplish this goal, but it creates other problems. On one side of the channel, the shifting sand piles up into a sand bar. On the other side of the channel, the sand continues to wash away, but no new sand replaces it. Slowly, that beachfront erodes.

Groins are the least destructive of the man-made barriers. They rely on the currents naturally shifting sand along the beach. Parallel rows of sand or small stones are built out into the water, perpendicular from the beach. Sand builds up on one side of the groin as it wears away on the other. In this way, as one groin is eroded away, another is built up, naturally, right next to it.

A jetty reaches into the ocean toward the top of this picture. The jetty blocked the natural movement of sand down the coastline, causing the beach in the foreground to erode.

On many beaches, houses are threatened by slowly rising tides. Those who place stone or steel break walls on the beaches in front of their homes are often protected. As the waves crash into them, water is projected back onto incoming waves. As a result of this washing action, the beach in front of the break wall erodes. As the beach in front of the wall slips away, the beaches on each side begin to erode as well. Neighbors on either side of a beach wall are affected—even if they do not have a break wall of their own.

In some communities, the entire shoreline is reinforced. As a result, all of the sand on the beach washes away. If the community wants to have a beach, it must spend hundreds of thousands of dollars each year to replenish its beaches. In the United States, the city of Virginia Beach spends $800,000 every year to have dump trucks haul sand for the tourist season. Virginia Beach is not alone. "Ten years ago, Ocean City, New Jersey, paid $5.2 million to replenish the beach; six months later it was gone," Steve Kemper states in his *Smithsonian* article.

A truck dumps sand onto a beach in Myrtle Beach, South Carolina. American cities spend millions of dollars each year to replace sand that has been washed away by the tides.

> This year, at an initial cost of $39 million, the process is starting all over again. Ocean City, Maryland, got a $14.2 million beach in 1988, spent another $25 million in 1990 and '91 for sand and a seawall, lost its protective dune and part of its beach last winter, and spent another $12 million for more sand this past summer.

Some cities replenish their beaches by dredging nearby canals or marina waterways and then pumping the recovered sand onto the beach. This is not the safest practice, however. Experts estimate that 10 percent of these dredgings are polluted with oil, gas, and partially treated sewage that find their way into harbors from marinas and coastal communities.

Limits on coastal building

The Coastal Barrier Resources Act (CBRA) discourages rampant coastal building in the United States. Passed in 1982, it protects 186 undeveloped islands, spits, and beaches along the Atlantic and Gulf coasts from development. Though people can build in these areas, no federal funds may be used for roads, bridges, or flood insurance. Essentially, this act shifts costs—and risks—of building in coastal areas from the federal taxpayers to the private landowners.

Other provisions were added to the CBRA in 1990. States with shorelines were encouraged to add provisions of their own. Though many states, like Georgia, have few restrictions on coastal building, others, like North Carolina and Michigan, added "setback laws." These setback laws have come to be called fall-back or fall-in laws. They require new building to be beyond a designated erosion line. This designation takes into account future erosion as well as the number of people who will likely use the coastal region. The setback requirement is greater for multifamily or commercial buildings, condos or hotels, for example, than for private, single-family homes.

This provision also does not allow homes damaged in storms or floods to be rebuilt unless the location is within the designated setback area. Barriers, such as break walls,

A sign announces that a stretch of coastal wetlands in South Padre Island, Texas, is for sale. Once purchased, the land will likely be developed, and the wetlands will be destroyed.

jetties, groins, or piers, which can worsen erosion in other places, are not allowed to be newly built or replaced.

Without government support for the building of barriers, a few individuals have taken matters into their own hands. Rodman D. Griffin reports for the *CQ Researcher:*

> On Galveston Bay, for example, desperate ranchers have positioned junked cars on the shore to prevent the waters from washing away roads. In Louisiana, shrimpers use wire mesh and old tires to keep the bay waters from chewing away at their bluffs. On Long Island, beach residents shore up dunes with driftwood and old tires.

Some experts believe that if local governments discourage further coastal development the populations at the coasts might then retreat. Other experts doubt this is likely. They point to the rebuilding that occurs after the devastation of tropical storms and hurricanes as proof that nothing will cause people to stay away from the coasts.

Toll on the coastline

Even natural wetlands that are protected are not entirely out of danger. Piers, groins, and break walls built in nearby coastal communities have the same erosive effects to wetlands as they do to beaches. Wetlands are capable of withstanding the rising and lowering of their water levels with the tides, but erosion could weaken the habitat. This is already happening in the southern United States. In Louisiana, erosion of the coast has allowed saltwater to flow into the inland freshwater wetlands. The saltwater is killing marsh grasses and endangering fisheries. The effects on the ecosystem could be devastating. Across the delta of the Mississippi River, freshwater marsh grasses hold the soil in place. According to Griffin:

> While coastal erosion is a problem for most coastal states, it is a veritable crisis for Louisiana. Along a broad expanse of southern Louisiana, between the Atchafalaya and Mississippi rivers, a million acres of coastal wetlands have disappeared since 1990.

Geologists estimate that many Louisiana counties could be swallowed by the ocean within five to ten years. This would be a disaster not only for Louisiana but also for the United States as a whole. Forty percent of the nation's coastal wetlands are located in Louisiana.

A need for compromise

Countries with developed coastlines have only recently learned the dangers of reshaping coastal land. Many developing nations are now beginning to build on their coastlines. The lure of tourist income is great for these mostly poor countries, yet the lessons of richer nations are clear. If development is not curbed, not only coastal habitat but also the entire ocean will be affected. The majority of marine life and some of the planet's most important ecosystems hug the coasts of the global ocean. If humans want to remain within the coastal zone, they need to focus on changes that will benefit both human and marine life. Many agencies and special interest groups are finding ways to make this possible.

6

The Ocean's Future

TAKING STEPS TO reverse what humans have done to the ocean is as daunting as the ocean is vast. Much of the ocean has already been polluted. Cleaning it up takes a great deal of time, money, and effort. At the same time, new ways of handling waste must be found so that further pollution can be avoided. Methods also are needed to curb overfishing while continuing to provide adequate protein for nations dependent on seafood. Plans for coastal development need to include consideration for the effects the proposed action will have on coastal habitats and the wildlife these habitats support. Complicating these efforts is the fact that people do not yet understand how all the parts of the global ocean interact. "We know as little about much of the ocean as we do about the moon," states marine scientist Sylvia Earle.

Another challenge facing those who wish to preserve the ocean is the need to gain international cooperation. The global ocean is a resource shared by many countries. Actions taken by one nation, or even by a few, will not protect the entire ocean. Through its treaties, the United Nations has played a vital role in getting all nations to participate in the protection of the ocean.

One of the most significant actions taken by the United Nations came in 1981 when all UN countries having ocean coastlines agreed to honor MARPOL, the international marine pollution treaty. This historic document contains many provisions to protect the global ocean. For example, Annex V of the treaty prohibits the discharging of waste or

This mound of garbage washed onto the beach represents a small portion of the pollution dumped into the ocean every year.

other chemicals into the ocean and the dumping of all plastics. It also limits the type of garbage that ships can legally dump on the open sea. Since it was passed in 1981, it has helped lower the amount of ocean pollution. By banning the flushing of oil residue out of holding tanks, MARPOL has reduced the amount of oil entering the ocean by 1 million tons since 1981.

The responsibility of enforcing UN treaties falls to the member nations. Unfortunately, not all of these nations are willing or able to make sure the treaties are followed. For one thing, many countries lack the resources to police the oceans. They simply cannot afford the high cost of finding and capturing those who violate the treaties. Other nations have the resources to back up the treaties, but they lack the political enthusiasm to do so. Nations that are politically hostile, or even at war, are not likely to cooperate on the enforcement of a treaty, no matter how important it is.

When nations do not cooperate to enforce a treaty, resentment can build up between them. For example, many developed countries are spending a great deal of money to improve sewage treatment. The leaders of these nations begin to resent undeveloped nations that are not spending as much money to clean up the environment. The rich nations may even place restrictions, such as trade embargoes, on the less developed nations. At the same time, the poorer nations may resent the rich nations for penalizing them for simply not having the resources to live up to the treaties.

Some nations take the MARPOL treaty seriously and enforce it aggressively. France is one such nation. French customs officers, using two twin-engine aircraft, watch for violations of Annex V within that nation's EEZ. Equipped with a video camera, the French officers not only monitor ships that dump waste at sea, but also record proof of the violations. The aircraft are high tech. Infrared sensors scan the area beneath the aircraft for evidence of sewage dumping. Side-mounted radar detects hydrocarbon spills within a twenty-one-mile (thirty-five-kilometer) radius. Hydrocarbon spills would indicate the release of gasoline or industrial waste chemicals such as methane, benzene, or acetylene. In addition to recording evidence for use in court, violators are arrested. Penalties include fines, jail time, or both.

Fish cops

The MARPOL treaty also includes sections designed to prevent overfishing. Again, enforcement is required in order to make the treaty work. This is a problem of special concern for developing nations that have neither the naval fleets nor the money to patrol coastal waters. Some nations join together with their neighbors or with countries that have permission to fish in their waters to try to stop poachers. Sometimes the confrontations turn violent.

During the mid-1990s an Argentine gunboat chased and fired at a Taiwanese trawler that was poaching the waters off the coast of Patagonia. The crew was rescued even though the trawler sank. In another case, Russian border-guard ships fired on two Japanese vessels, damaging one ship and injuring several fishermen. The fishermen were accused of poaching in disputed waters off the Kuril Islands. In the South Atlantic, a Falklands patrol boat chased a Taiwanese squid boat for thirteen days before losing it. "We think shooting is excessive," reported a Falklands fisheries officer.

When nations cannot afford to enforce fishing laws themselves, they must look for alternatives to protect their ocean resources. In Sierra Leone, for example, traditional fishers found that they were barely able to catch enough fish to feed local people because foreign trawlers were depleting the fish stock. The government established a five-mile zone along the coastline limited to traditional fishers. Commercial trawlers were allowed to fish only the waters outside this five-mile zone. Worldwatch research associate Peter Weber stated:

> Because the country lacked the resources to patrol the commercial fishing waters, it established a self-policing policy under which one foreign-based company issued the fishing licenses and enforced fishing regulations. Under this experiment, the number of foreign boats fell from around 170 to 50, and poaching fell off due to constant patrols.

A Mexican trawler sails across the Sea of Cortez. The activities of fishing vessels worldwide are regulated under the MARPOL treaty, which was adopted by the UN in 1981.

Foreign fishing concerns are not the only violators of the MARPOL treaty. Nations must also enforce fishing regulations among their own fishermen. In the United States, fishing limits are enforced by a little-known agency, the National Marine Fisheries Service (NMFS). Every year 112 NMFS agents monitor, mediate, and enforce laws protecting fisheries and endangered marine species. Called fish cops, they work on both land and water, often with the assistance of local law enforcement officers. The task is huge and, as TV producer and environmental writer David Helvarg recently pointed out, thankless: "Fish cops are criticized for not doing enough by their allies in the environmental movement and pressured to do less by the industries they monitor."

The NMFS agents not only protect marine life from the perils of overfishing, but they also protect consumers from dangerous products. In one operation, the NMFS agents watched a group of Massachusetts fishermen dig clams from a mudflat contaminated with sewage. There was nothing illegal about this activity, as long as the clams were used only for fishing bait. This was not what the fishermen had in mind, however. They sold the contaminated clams to local restaurants. The NMFS moved in, arrested the fishermen, and confiscated the clams. Laboratory tests showed that the clams contained 80 percent more contaminants than the law allows—enough to cause illness.

Sustainable fishing

As the Massachusetts clam dig shows, some fishermen are willing to break the law if they believe the profits are great enough. That is why one of the world's largest seafood producers, Unilever, has taken a different approach to saving future fish stocks. The European-based company believes that it can help curtail poaching and overfishing by making it more profitable to obey the law than to break it. Unilever has proposed that an identifiable seal or label be placed on all seafood products caught and manufactured for them. They are convinced this discourages wasteful fishing practices and protects the ocean environment for the future. Seafood will only be purchased by Unilever from fishermen who can prove that they are *not* overfishing, fishing in illegal areas, or using harmful fishing gear.

Teaming with the Worldwide Fund for Nature, an environmental group, Unilever will share the cost to set up this system. The team hopes the labeling program will encourage the kind of fishing that will allow the fishing stock to mature and replenish itself. This type of fishing is known as sustainable fishing. Unilever is using profit incentives to convince fishermen that sustainable fishing is more profitable than overfishing or fishing that generates wasteful bycatch.

Another alternative to controlling overfishing is the creation of fishing zones. With fishing zones, areas are set aside where fish are allowed to mature and reproduce. This helps ensure that fish stocks will replenish themselves. At the same time, the natural habitat of these no-fishing zones is left untouched, which is an added plus for the ocean environment. New Zealand was one of the first nations to pioneer the use of no-fishing zones.

Fish farming or mariculture

Some people believe that the long-term solution to overfishing is to eliminate traditional fishing altogether and replace it with something else—aquaculture. These people compare fishing to hunting on land. In both activities, wild creatures are pursued through their natural habitat, are caught, and are killed for food. For thousands of years, people have known that it is safer, more sanitary, and more profitable to capture animals, allow them to breed, and then harvest them rather than chase them across the land and kill them one by one. In this way, agriculture has replaced hunting as the main source of meat and protein. Proponents of fish farming, or aquaculture, believe the process should be repeated in the ocean. Fish should be captured and raised in a controlled environment, then harvested without damaging the environment.

Fish farming involves setting aside shoreline waters to create breeding ponds. Fish larvae are grown in tanks to a specific size before being released into the ponds. So far,

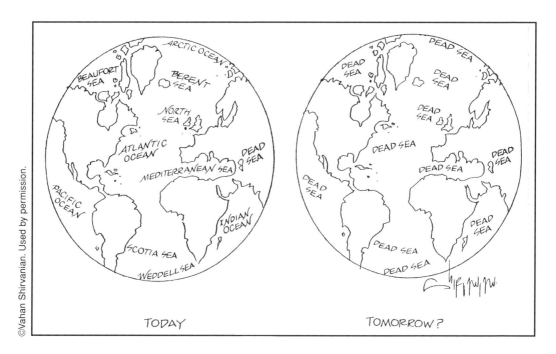

TODAY · TOMORROW?

the ocean species that have done best are salmon and halibut. Seventy percent of salmon purchased today by consumers comes from fish farms, predominantly in Scotland and Norway. Aquaculture accounts for nearly 20 percent of the total fish on the market today.

Fish farming is not without its problems. At first, fish farmers crowded too many fish into their ponds. Disease and sea lice quickly spread among the fish stock. Once the problem was solved, healthier fish were harvested. This caused another problem. The market was flooded with farm-grown fish, causing prices to fall. This problem was corrected with better management of fish harvesting and marketing.

To make fish farming viable for more species, some experts believe that farming needs to move away from the shores to the open seas. Fish farming in the open sea, known as mariculture, would allow the breeding or "growing" of a greater variety of species, such as red snapper, striped bass, and mahimahi.

The greatest deterrents to mariculture have been fear of shark attacks and the plundering of the fish stock by sea lions and other marine species. John Ericsson, an inventor and president of Sea Pride, believes he has solved these problems. Ericsson has designed large, fiberglass cages that extend into the water from a platform similar to those used for drilling oil. The lightweight barriers keep predators out, are easily cleaned, and can be lifted from the water to harvest the fish.

Mariculture may be even better for the global ocean than aquaculture is, because valuable coastlines do not have to be destroyed to create breeding areas. In Ecuador, for example, fish farmers have converted mangrove forests into shrimp ponds. The effect on the coastal ecosystem, however, has been devastating. Because the shrimp industry generates an average of $500 million a year, a sizable amount of Ecuador's export income, the Ecuadorian government does not want to shut down the operation. Instead, the government now trains shrimp farmers to protect the coastal environment, while continuing to farm the shrimp ponds.

Computer-aided solutions

Disasters like the one in Ecuador could be avoided if governments and commercial operations would make use of all the tools now available for managing ocean resources. As in so many other areas, computers can be useful to track trends and make predictions about the future of the global ocean. Computer forecasting programs can simulate currents, tides, coastal alteration, temperature, and other factors and their effects on one another. By entering current data on, for example, plans to develop an area of coast of a Third World country, the program can simulate the repercussions that construction and alteration will have on coastal erosion, currents, tides, and wildlife resources.

Using a computer, scientists can estimate how the manufacture of a coastal wetland will influence water quality, global temperature, coastal erosion, neighboring countries, or the ocean in general. If a solution causes greater damage or new problems in the future, it can be altered before it is carried out.

Computers are also being used to spread the message about how the ocean is affected by the actions of people living inland. Information about what damage various types of pollution cause to the ocean, how they enter the ocean, or about the potential dangers of different programs to coastal wetlands and wildlife is available to the general public, largely through the use of the Internet. Satellites, too, help improve communication by getting information to the public faster through the news media.

Bioremediation

Scientists are also seeking high-tech solutions to the problem of ocean pollution. Some of the discoveries made so far hold a great deal of promise for the future of the ocean. For example, a British company has found a way to turn one kind of pollution against another kind.

The firm, Biotechna, has designed a method for algae to purify sewage. Scientists know that when sewage is released into ocean water, the algae in the water starts to feed on it, drawing in all its nutrients. Normally, this begins a cycle that can lead to eutrophication, or the condition whereby the feeding organisms consume all the oxygen. As the tiny organisms feed, they become overstimulated and begin to multiply at an excessive rate. The water soon becomes polluted by algal blooms that rob the water of oxygen. Biotechna has found a way not only to harness this activity, but also to break down the pollution without robbing the water of oxygen. "We're just doing what nature does—but we're controlling it," Stephen Skill of Biotechna has stated. Together with colleague Lee Robinson, Skill developed the Biocoil tank, which uses algae to break down sewage before it is released into the ocean. Algae eat 95 percent of the ammonia and nitrates and 90 percent of the phosphates. One Biocoil tank purifies the amount of sewage generated by a town of twenty-five hundred people.

The process of using nature to purify waste is called biotreatment or bioremediation. Scientists have found that not only algae, but many other organisms can be implemented

Developed by Biotechna, a private firm, the Bio-coil tank uses algae to break down sewage.

to purify and process waste and even to eat toxic chemicals. Since the process uses microbes found in nature, the end product is organic in nature. Sometimes the purified waste can be used as fertilizer.

In the United States, for example, at least twenty waste treatment sites are using microbes to convert waste into a mulchlike soil conditioner. One of these sites is operated by the Palm Beach County Solid Waste Authority in Florida. The processing facility cost $1.3 million to build and handles thirty tons of sewage, sludge, and yard clippings a day. "The result, 21 days later, is an almost odorless, fluffy soil conditioner that the county uses on its own parklands and sells to garden shops," James D. Snyder, author and editor in the field of industrial environmental management, has reported.

Bioremediation is also being used to clean up more than two hundred toxic landfills located in the United States. These toxins will be broken down by the microbes and will be less likely to leak into the ocean through rain runoff or end up in groundwater supplies that eventually lead into the ocean. Test sites for oil-eating microbes were used in the *Exxon Valdez* spill, and naturally occurring microbes have begun to clean up the oil spilled into the Persian Gulf during the Gulf War.

Australia's Great Barrier Reef

One of the traditional measures countries have used to preserve a wild habitat is to turn the area into a preserve or natural park. Most of the world's national parks are on land, but some nations have applied the concept to areas in the ocean. The track record for using this method to protect ocean habitats, however, is not encouraging. According to Peter Weber, "Although 65 countries worldwide have designated some 300 parks that include coral reefs, these are largely 'paper parks' without the funds or staff to protect [the] reef sufficiently." Australia is an exception to this rule. The island nation's management of its Great Barrier Reef Park serves as an example of how to manage an offshore park for the benefit of people and the environment.

Scientists estimated that the Great Barrier Reef is between 500,000 and 2,500,000 years old. Growing in large, broken sections along Australia's northeastern coast, it was threatened by pollution from the coast and from human contact and fishing exploitation. To protect it from continued damage, the Australian government designated the reef a national park in 1975.

Australia designated parts of the reef for specific uses. One area was set aside for scientific research, another for commercial fishing, and another for tourism, with sections also entirely restricted from human contact. All sections of the reef are patrolled and monitored by the Great Barrier Reef Marine Park Authority.

Though many marine specialists and environmentalists see the Great Barrier Reef Park as a model and encourage others to follow and adapt their protection policies in order to preserve other marine habitats, others disagree. Critics say the zone management of the reef and the cost to maintain and patrol it does not transfer to smaller coral reefs. Local management of reefs by the coastal communities may work better than creating a national park. Local people are familiar with a specific reef and how it has been damaged or exploited; they can best determine how to protect coastal reefs, according to the critics.

Think globally, act locally

The destruction of ocean ecosystems does not just happen. It is caused by the actions of people. Even small things can contribute to this worldwide problem. However, since people have created the problem, they also have the power to solve it. To do so, everyone must be aware of how the actions they take at the local level will influence the entire planet. That is why environment groups coined the slogan Think globally, act locally. A good example of how this kind of thinking can bring about change can be seen in the cleanup of Chesapeake Bay.

In 1978, the Chesapeake Bay Commission, formed of both individuals and special interest groups, won a lawsuit against the state of Maryland and the Environmental Protection Agency (EPA) to limit sewage pollution dumped into the bay and its supporting rivers and streams. Controlling pollution filtering into the bay is only one part of a three-part plan to bring the bay back from decline. The other points target not only the deterioration of the bay's fisheries, but also the restoration of the bay's natural resilience or buffer zones of aquatic plants, wetlands, and oyster beds.

According to Bernie Fowler, Maryland state senator and former chairman of the Chesapeake Bay Commission:

> You wonder how we let it go. You know, you hear people say the water seems cloudy, and I wonder what's happened to all the hardheads [fish]. The fishing fell off. The bay grasses disappeared. You notice all these things, but it comes so slow.

Progress comes slowly, too. Targets were set to be met by the year 2000. To encourage people to become involved, and to measure the success in a fun way, a "toes test" takes place every year. Tom Horton writes in his 1993 article in *National Geographic:*

> Every second Sunday in June, people from around the state of Maryland wade into the Patuxent [River] on Bernie Fowler Day. They are hoping to see their toes in the river, just as Bernie did as a young man in the 1950s.

Recent toes tests have progressed to thigh-deep levels; there has been progress.

Because of the cleanup campaign, individuals like Sherman Haas, a farmer in Pennsylvania, are doing their part to make sure they are not fouling the bay. "We do have a problem. But you wonder if your farm can be hurting Chesapeake Bay as bad as some say," Haas has said. To be on the safe side, Haas works with a professor of agronomy to balance the nutrient levels from his farm that end up in the surrounding watershed feeding Chesapeake Bay. Horton additionally has reported:

> In an effort not to add to the bay's troubles, Haas is trying to send out no more nutrients than he takes in. For that reason, he weighs every pig, every bag of feed and fertilizer, every truckload of hay, livestock bedding, and manure leaving and entering his operation.

A polluted wildlife refuge on Chesapeake Bay. Local cleanup efforts have reduced the amount of pollution in the bay.

Slow progress, but progress nonetheless

Even when citizens are concerned, however, the solutions to pollution problems are not always clear. For example, farmers in Pennsylvania thought they could help the cleanup of Chesapeake Bay by ending the use of chemical fertilizers. Instead of chemicals, they used manure to enrich their soil. They were dismayed to find out, however, that the runoff from their land actually contained more phosphorus and nitrogen when it was fertilized with manure than it had when it was fertilized with chemicals.

Despite setbacks like these, progress is being made. Chesapeake Bay is just one example of what individual efforts and widespread cooperation can accomplish. The key to the slow but steady progress is in spreading the word. People need to understand their role in polluting the ocean before they will curtail their actions.

The experience gained at Chesapeake Bay proves that even damage to an ocean ecosystem can be undone. The global ocean possesses an amazing ability to restore itself, but humankind must help. People must continue to look for new ways to manage the ocean's resources, particularly those that will benefit both humankind and the ocean habitat. Progress is underway—one bay, one coral reef, one coastal wetland, and one species of endangered marine life at a time.

Glossary

aquaculture: Using inland ponds or pens along the ocean coastline to breed and grow fish and other seafood.

bioremediation: Treating contaminated or polluted areas of soil or water by using bacteria and microorganisms that eat pollutants.

bycatch: Unavoidable by-product of fishing; other species of fish caught in the net and then discarded.

buoy: A floating object that marks a channel or something underwater.

coastal zone: An area along the coastline including the entire coastal plain above the water line and the continental shelf below the water line.

commercial extinction: The point at which the cost to harvest a species outweighs its commercial value due to its limited numbers.

continental shelf: A gently sloping area from the beach to the drop-off into deeper ocean terrain.

copepods: Tiny crustaceans that are an important food source for most marine animals.

coral reef: Marine animals growing in tropical waters that support a variety of marine life as part of their ecosystem.

ecosystem: A group of living plants and animals that rely on each other for food and shelter. They survive because of their relationship to each other and with the nonliving things in their environment, such as soil and climate conditions.

eutrophication: An accumulation of nutrients that causes rapid growth of algae, which, in turn, depletes the water of oxygen.

Exclusive Economic Zone (EEZ): An area up to two hundred nautical miles from shore within which each nation has exclusive rights to seafood and marine resources.

estuarine wetland: A coastal or saltwater wetland.

estuary: A wetland area formed by a widening at the mouth of a river where the river meets the ocean.

finfish: A group of marine animals that use fins to swim in the ocean.

gill net: An unattended drift net woven of fine mesh placed near shore and anchored to rocks or buoys for catching fish.

groundfish: A bottom-dwelling finfish such as mackerel, red snapper, or redfish.

mangrove forest: A type of wetland that grows along coastlines, containing mainly trees that thrive in water.

mariculture: Using cages in the open sea to breed and grow ocean species of fish and other seafood.

nonpoint pollution: Pollution such as air particles and runoff from roadways that is difficult to trace to a specific source.

open ocean: The area of ocean beyond the two-hundred-mile limit of the Exclusive Economic Zone.

overfishing: The practice of catching more fish of a certain species than necessary to ensure only those go to market that are largest and will bring the best price; others are thrown overboard as part of the bycatch.

photoplankton: A tiny marine plant that is an important food and supplier of oxygen for marine animals.

salt marsh: A type of wetland occurring along coastlines that contains hardy plants and bushes that thrive in the saltwater brought in by tides.

shellfish: Shell-covered marine animals, also called crustaceans, which are harvested for food; for example, oysters, clams, crabs, and lobsters.

trawling net: A funnel-shaped net that is dragged along the bottom of the ocean to catch seafood.

wetland: An ecosystem containing plants, trees, and animals that thrive in wet or muddy conditions; wetlands filter pollution and serve as breeding grounds for many fish, birds, and animals.

Organizations
to Contact

American Oceans Campaign
725 Arizona Ave., Suite 102
Santa Monica, CA 90401
(310) 576-6162
fax: (310) 576-6170

American Oceans Campaign's mission is to preserve and protect marine ecosystems. Through education programs targeted to the public and key decision makers, it strives to stop ocean pollution. It helped ban the use of drift nets in American waters. American Oceans Campaign publishes many brochures and the magazine *Splash*, issued four times a year.

Center for Marine Conservation
1725 DeSales St. NW, Suite 600
Washington, DC 20036
(202) 429-5609
fax: (202) 872-0619

Originally named Center for Environmental Education, the Center for Marine Conservation focuses on protecting not only marine habitats and wildlife, but also coastal and ocean resources. The center conducts programs to clean up beaches, to keep plastics out of the water, and to prevent fishing gear and garbage from entangling or suffocating marine animals. It publishes *Marine Conservation News* four times per year and *Coastal Connection* twice a year.

Coast Alliance
215 Pennsylvania Ave. SE, 3rd Floor
Washington, DC 20003
(202) 546-9554
fax: (202) 546-9609

Coast Alliance is a group of coastal activists working to raise awareness of resources available on the coasts of the oceans and the Great Lakes.

Cousteau Society, Inc.
870 Greenbrier Circle, Suite 402
Chesapeake, VA 23320
(757) 523-9335
fax: (757) 523-2747

Through sponsorship of scientific research of the ocean depths and marine life, the Cousteau Society strives to improve the quality of the ocean for the present and the future. Books and television programs on marine life help to educate the public about the ocean, its resources, and the need for conservation of both.

Environmental Protection Agency (EPA)
Office of Wetlands, Oceans, and Watersheds
401 M St. SW
Washington, DC 20460
(202) 260-7751
fax: (202) 260-6294

The EPA, a federal agency, protects marine and estuary environments. It creates general environmental regulations, which are enforced through regional offices.

Marine Science Institute
500 Discovery Pkwy.
Redwood City, CA 94063-4746
(650) 364-2760
fax: (650) 364-0416

Founded in 1970 to promote environmental awareness and marine science education, the Marine Science Institute conducts several education programs and a Discovery Voyage through schools and colleges.

National Oceanographic and Atmospheric Administration (NOAA)

Department of Commerce
Office of Public Affairs
Washington, DC 20230
(202) 482-2985
fax: (202) 482-3154

Established in 1970 to bring together several agencies working for the betterment of the environment, the agencies under the NOAA's control include the National Ocean Service, the National Marine Fisheries Service, the Hazardous Material Response Branch, and the National Environmental Satellite and Data and Information Service (NESDIS). The NOAA supports an extensive marine pollution library collection. The library can be reached at (301) 443-8330.

Websites

The Globe Program

http://www.globe.gov/

An international environmental science and education partnership designed to increase environmental awareness. Students participate in the Global Learning and Observation to Benefit the Environment (GLOBE) using projects and activities to make observations and report their data via the Web. Scientists use the data for research. Students, teachers, and friends of the environment may participate.

National Marine Fisheries Service (NMFS)

http://kingfish.ssp.nmfs.gov

Part of the National Oceanic and Atmospheric Administration (NOAA), the NMFS administers the management and conservation of the nation's fisheries. This site offers some audio clips, the latest fishery statistics, information on marine law enforcement, a link to their 125th anniversary page, and search capabilities of the agency's valuable databases of information.

Ocean Planet
http://seawifs.gsfc.nasa.gov/ocean_planet.html

An on-line floor plan with "rooms" to visit that highlights items from this Smithsonian traveling exhibit. The "oceans in peril" room connects to buoys with pages linking information on ocean pollution, waste, habitats, fishing, and planet-wide topics. Contains some links to other websites as well.

Wired for Conservation
http://www.tnc.org

Home page for the Nature Conservancy, this website provides information on endangered species, highlights of conservation efforts, nature chats, and informative articles with links and photos on a variety of conservation science topics.

Woods Hole Oceanographic Institution (WHOI)
http://www.whoi.edu/index.html

Scientists at WHOI have been studying the ocean for sixty-five years. They are world leaders in oceanography. This website has general information, visitor information, research, education, and resources available including video animations.

Suggestions for Further Reading

John Christopher Fine, *Oceans in Peril*. New York: Atheneum, 1987.

Martha Gorman, *Environmental Hazards: Marine Pollution*. Santa Barbara, CA: ABC-CLIO, 1993.

Anita Louise McCormick, *Vanishing Wetlands*. San Diego: Lucent Books, 1995.

Christina G. Miller and Louise A. Berry, *Coastal Rescue: Preserving Our Seashores*. New York: Atheneum, 1989.

Don Nardo, *Oil Spills*. San Diego: Lucent Books, 1990.

April Pulley Sayre, *Exploring Earth's Biomes: Ocean*. New York: Twenty First Century Books, 1996.

Jenny Tesar, *Threatened Oceans*. New York: Facts On File, 1991.

Works Consulted

Rachel Carson, *The Sea Around Us*. New York: Oxford University Press, 1951.

Merritt Clifton, "Driftnets: Scourge of the Seas," *Animals' Agenda*, October 1989.

Congressional Quarterly Weekly Report, "Ocean Dumping Law Targets Vessels," February 8, 1992.

Tucker Coombe, "Beach Sweeping and Ocean Keeping," *Sea Frontiers*, July/August 1993.

Mariette DiChristina, "Sea Power," *Popular Science*, May 1995.

Economist, "Alaskan Fishing: Pollock Overboard," January 6, 1996.

Futurist, "More People, Fewer Fish," May/June 1996.

Rodman D. Griffin, "Threatened Coastlines," *CQ Researcher*, February 7, 1992.

David Helvarg, "When Uncle Sam's 'Fish Cops' Reel in a Suspect, He's Usually a Keeper," *Smithsonian*, February 1997.

Don Hinrichsen, "Coasts in Crisis," *Issues in Science & Technology*, vol. 12, no. 4, Summer 1996.

Tom Horton, "Chesapeake Bay—Hanging in the Balance," *National Geographic*, June 1993.

International Agricultural Development, "Fisheries: Overfishing Nets Disaster," May/June 1995.

Steve Kemper, "This Beach Boy Sings a Song Developers Don't Want to Hear," *Smithsonian*, October 1992.

Tom Knudson, "Waste on a Grand Scale Loots Sea," *Sacramento Bee*, December 11, 1995.

Bill Lawren, "Net Loss," *National Wildlife*, October/November 1992.

Gary Lee, "Heeding the Seas' Vanishing Species," *Washington Post*, April 1, 1996.

Beth Livermore, "Fishing for Cures," *Popular Science*, May 1995.

Jon McBeth, "But There's a Catch . . . ," *Far Eastern Economic Review*, May 16, 1996.

Anne Platt McGinn, "A Private-Sector Sustainable Fishing Initiative," *World Watch*, September/October 1996.

Sy Montgomery, "A Deadly New Wave of Cyanide Fishing," *Animals*, January/February 1996.

Marjorie L. Mooney-Seus and George S. Stone, "The Big Ones Are Getting Away," *Sea Frontiers*, Fall 1995.

Madhusree Mukerjee, "Fish Fight," *Scientific American*, October 1996.

National Geographic, "Bones of the Sea, Coral Mends the Human Frame," Earth Almanac, March 1992.

National Geographic, "A Glowing Success: Using Algae as Purifiers," Earth Almanac, March 1994.

National Geographic, "New Chemical Digs Deep into *Exxon Valdez* Oil," Earth Almanac, August 1994.

National Geographic, "Undersea Graffiti at Corals' Expense," Earth Almanac, January 1997.

National Geographic, "Walls of Death, Drift Nets Will Kill No More," Earth Almanac, April 1992.

Michael Parfit, "Diminishing Returns: Exploiting the Ocean's Bounty," *National Geographic*, November 1995.

Joseph Raulinaitis, "FDA Goes Fishing for Toxic Waste," *FDA Consumer*, March 1994.

Michael Satchell, "The Rape of the Oceans," *U.S. News & World Report*, June 22, 1992.

Science News, "Fishing: What We Don't Keep," December 16, 1995.

Libby Smith, "Let's Not Go Overboard!" *Conservationist*, July 1990.

James D. Snyder, "Off-the-Shelf Bugs Hungrily Gobble Our Nastiest Pollutants," *Smithsonian*, April 1993.

Richard Stone, "Swimming Against the PCB Tide," *Science*, February 1992.

Michael Tennesen, "Kelp: Keeping a Forest Afloat," *National Wildlife*, June/July 1992.

James Tobin, "Sea Coral Bone Graft Gives Teen Chance at Being a Kid Again," *Detroit News*, December 22, 1996.

UNESCO Courier, "Marine Pollution: Something to Declare," February 1995.

Michael Weber, "Oceans at Risk," *Popular Science*, May 1995.

Michael Weber and Judith A. Gradwohl, *The Wealth of Oceans*. New York: W. W. Norton, 1995.

Peter Weber, *Abandoned Seas: Reversing the Decline of the Oceans*. Washington, DC: Worldwatch Institute, 1993.

———, "Coral Reefs Face the Threat of Extinction," *USA Today*, May 1993.

———, "It Comes Down to the Coasts," *World Watch*, March/April 1994.

———, "Reversing the Decline of Oceans," *USA Today*, September 1994.

Index

Abu Ali Peninsula, 46
Africa, 9, 15, 60
Alaska. *See Exxon Valdez*
algae, 55, 56, 75–76
American Oceans
  Campaign, 84
Antarctic Peninsula, 45
aquaculture, 72–73
Arctic Ocean, 8, 13
Asia, 8, 60
Atlantic Ocean, 8, 43, 53,
  54, 64
Australia, 9, 14, 15

Barents Sea, 51
bays, 42–43
beaches, 62–63
  efforts to clean, 40
Bering Strait, 8
biological oxygen demand
  (BOD), 42–43
bioremediation, 75–77
Biotechna, 75
birds. *See* seabirds
buoys, 10
bycatch, 27–29, 72
  regulation of, 30–31

Canada, 29, 36
  see also Grand Banks
    fishery
Center for Marine Conservation, 10, 40, 84

chemicals, 6
  deep ocean dumping of,
    50–51
  pollute oceans, 38, 46–48,
    49
Chesapeake Bay, 43, 78–80
China, 15, 57
Coastal Barrier Resources
  Act (CBRA), 63–64
Coast Alliance, 85
coastal zone, 54
  building on, 63–66
  erosion of, 61–63, 65
  mangrove forests found in,
    60–61
cod, New England, 32, 33
continental shelf, 54, 55
coral, 7, 55
  used for bone grafts, 19
coral reefs, 14, 55–58, 61
  see also Great Barrier Reef
Cousteau Society, 85
crustaceans, 55
currents, ocean, 9–10
  causes of, 11–12, 14
  used for hydroelectricity,
    22

DDT, 47–48
Delaware River, 45
Dulcie Atoll, 38
Dutch, use of wetlands by,
  60

eagles, 45
ecosystems
  in coastal waters, 55, 58,
    65, 74
  global, 14–15
  ocean, 13–14
    damage to, 24, 28–29, 42,
      55
    from ship ballast, 52–53
  see also coral reefs
Ecuador, 19, 61, 74
endangered species
  living in wetlands, 59
Environmental Protection
  Agency, 85
Europe, 12
European Union, 29
eutrophication, 42–43
Exclusive Economic Zone
  (EEZ), 29, 35, 69
Exxon Valdez, 44–45, 77

fish, 61
  commercial extinction of,
    32–33
  in coral reefs, 56–57
  harvesting new species of,
    33–34
Fisheries Conservation and
  Management Act of 1976,
  29
fishing industry, 25–28
  damages ocean ecosystems,
    28–29
  is needed for jobs, 31–33
  regulation of, 29–31,
    36–37, 69–72
  see also aquaculture;
    bycatch; mariculture;
    poaching
floating factories, 26–27

France, 69

Galveston Bay, 45, 65
garbage, 6, 51, 68
  dumping of, into oceans,
    38–41
gill nets, 36–37, 38
Grand Banks fishery, 31,
  34–35
gravel, 7, 20
Great Barrier Reef, 14,
  77–78
Great Lakes, 52–53, 54
Greenland, 8
guano, 18–19, 28
Gulf of Alaska, 44
Gulf of Mexico, 12, 54, 64
Gulf War, 45–46

Hussein, Saddam, 45–46
hydroelectricity, 22–23

India, 35–36
Indian Ocean, 9
Indonesia, 35

Japan, 15, 29
jellyfish, 20

Kara Sea, 51
kelp, 55
Kissimmee River, 60
Kuril Islands, 69
Kuwait, 46

limestone, 20–21
logging, 61

Magellan, Ferdinand, 9
magnesium, 20
Magnuson, Warren, 29

Magnuson Act, 29–31, 32
manatees, 61
manta rays, 27
mariculture, 73–74
marine biologists, 19
marine life, 6, 7
  chemicals are harmful to,
    46–48
  on coastal zone, 54
  efforts to preserve, 71
  killed by garbage, 40–41
  in mangrove forests, 61
  uses for, 17–19
    medical research, 19–20
  see also bycatch; fish;
    fishing industry
Marine Science Institute,
  85–86
MARPOL, 41, 43,
  treaty, 67–69, 71
Massachusetts Bay Industrial
  Waste Site, 50–51
medical research, 19–20
minerals, 7
  found in oceans, 20–21
Mississippi River, 65

National Coalition for
  Marine Conservation, 86
National Guard, 52
National Marine Fisheries
  Service, 10–11, 28
National Oceanographic and
  Atmospheric Administra-
  tion, 86
natural gas, 23–24
New England Fishery
  Management Council, 32
New Zealand, 72
Nike shoes, 10–11
North America, 8, 15

North Sea, 29
Norway, 73

ocean(s)
  are endangered, 6–7
  efforts to preserve, 67–69,
    74–80
  floor, 11–12
  mills, 21–22
  natural resources of, 15–19,
    23–24
    see also hydroelectricity;
      natural gas; oil
  research on, 20
  temperature, 11, 12, 22
  used for energy, 20–22
  see also currents, ocean;
    marine life; pollution;
    water; named oceans
oceanographers, 10
Ocean Thermal Energy
  Conversion, 22
octopus, 14, 56
oil, 6, 7, 51
  as natural resource, 23–24
  spills, 43–46
oysters, 18

Pacific Ocean, 8–9, 12, 38,
  54
Patagonia, 69
pearls, 18
Persian Gulf, 46, 77
Peru, 19, 28–29
phytoplankton, 55
poaching, 35, 69
pollock, 33–34
pollution, 6–7
  sources of, 48–49, 51–52
  see also chemicals; gar-
    bage; sewage

polychlorinated biphenyls
  (PCBs), 47–48
population, human, 7
  living in coastal zone,
    42, 54, 61, 65
Prince William Sound, 44

radioactive wastes, 50–51

salt, 16, 20
sand, 7, 20
sand eels, 29
Saudi Arabia, 46
Scotland, 73
seabirds, 18, 61
  hurt by pollution, 40, 41, 44
seafood
  provided by oceans, 15–16
sea lions, 17
seals, 17, 40
Sea of Cortez, 27
sea otters, 45, 61
Sea Pride, 74
seashells, 17–18
sea turtles, 40
sea urchins, 28, 56
seaweed, 16, 19, 55
sewage, 6
  problems caused by, 42–43
  treatment, 68
sharks, 14, 17, 19, 56
Shetland Islands, 29
ships. See vessels, oceangoing
shrimp, 28
Sierra Leone, 69
Sneaker Society, 10
South America, 8, 15, 60
Soviet Union, 51
sponges, 7, 55
  uses for, 17, 18, 19
squid, 27

St. Lawrence Seaway, 53
submarines, 24
sustainable fishing, 71–72

trawling, 25–27, 69, 70

unemployment
  due to fishing regulations,
    31–32
Unilever (corporation), 71–72
United Nations, 29, 51
  efforts to preserve oceans,
    67–68
  Food and Agricultural
    Organization, 27
United States, 15, 63–66
  dumps chemicals into
    oceans, 51
  efforts to control ocean
    pollution by, 40, 52–53,
    76
  rainfall in, 13
U.S. Navy, 39

vessels, oceangoing, 25–27,
  30
  cause oil pollution, 44
Virginia Beach, Virginia, 63

walruses, 17, 18
water
  amount of, on earth, 8–9
  evaporation of, 12–13
weather, 11–12
  causes of changes in, 14
wetlands, 61, 65–66
  benefit coastal zones,
    58–59
whales, 14, 17, 18

zooplankton, 55

Picture Credits

About the Author

Lisa A. Wroble is a professional freelance writer. She graduated cum laude from Eastern Michigan University with a B.A. in English language. While working as a publicist, and later as a technical writer, she began submitting articles to children's magazines. Ms. Wroble now has in print over one hundred articles for or about children. In addition, over a dozen of her articles have appeared in reference collections and textbooks. This book is her seventh, the first for Lucent Books. She most enjoys writing about history, psychology, the natural sciences, and the environment. Ms. Wroble lives in Michigan, where she spends her free time camping, boating, and photographing the outdoors.